Living in Union with Christ

Paul's Gospel and Christian Moral Identity

Grant Macaskill

Baker Academic

a division of Baker Publishing Group
Grand Rapids, Michigan

© 2019 by Grant Macaskill

Published by Baker Academic
a division of Baker Publishing Group
PO Box 6287, Grand Rapids, MI 49516-6287
www.bakeracademic.com

Paperback edition published 2023
ISBN 978-1-5409-6742-8

Printed in the United States of America

The Library of Congress has cataloged the hardcover edition as follows:
Names: Macaskill, Grant, author.
Title: Living in union with Christ : Paul's gospel and Christian moral identity / Grant Macaskill.
Description: Grand Rapids, MI : Baker Academic, a Division of Baker Publishing Group, [2019] | Includes bibliographical references and index.
Identifiers: LCCN 2019011772 | ISBN 9781540961242 (cloth)
Subjects: LCSH: Bible. Epistles of Paul—Criticism, interpretation, etc. | Christian life—Biblical teaching. | Mystical union—Biblical teaching.
Classification: LCC BS2655.C4 M34 2019 | DDC 227/.06—dc23
LC record available at https://lccn.loc.gov/2019011772

Cover image: Fresco from Debre Berhan Selassie Church (Gondar, Ethiopia) depicting the divine protection of the three youths in the furnace (Dan. 3). In Eastern tradition, their faithfulness is celebrated in this kontakion: "You did not worship the hand-graven image, O thrice-blessed ones, but armed with the immaterial [lit., ungraven] essence of God, you were glorified in a trial by fire" (Kontakion 6, trans. Grant Macaskill).

For Tom and Heather Greggs

Contents

Preface

Reconsidering Hope

This book is an exercise in the practical theological interpretation of Paul's Epistles. It involves careful exegesis of a number of passages in critical dialogue with the work of other biblical scholars, but its purpose is not simply to gain a better understanding of Paul's thought in its historical context, which is how biblical scholars often conceive of their task. Rather, it is ultimately oriented toward asking a practical theological question: As Christians who are committed to seeing Scripture as normative for our thought and practice, how then must we think and act today?

It is a book about hope—the hope of the gospel, and the hope that this gospel really does bring about freedom from the power of sin to control and destroy our lives. And it is about the *personal* character of this hope, by which I mean that it is constituted by a person who makes himself present with and in us to deliver us from sin. That person, Jesus Christ, is not just the one who brings us hope; he *is* our hope. The emphasis of this last statement can be shifted subtly in a way that further draws out its meaning: *he* is our hope. The possibilities of our lives are limited not by our own natural capacity for goodness and love but by the perfections and prospects constituted by this other person, Jesus Christ. Thanks be to God.

This personal hope should be at the center of the life and teaching of every church, displacing all other ways of thinking about God and what it means to walk with him. No element of Christian life or thought can be considered without reference to it and to the person in whom it is constituted. Behind my writing this book, though, lies a sense that the significance we attach to this personal hope has been reduced or truncated in ways that compromise the life of the church: it still shapes the way we think about forgiveness but does not adequately shape the way we think about Christian discipleship and growth.

To put this claim in the starkest of terms, the way we think about Christian morality—even within those parts of the church that self-identify as "evangelical"—is often functionally Christless. Too frequently, when we think about Christians as moral agents who act within the church and the world in an ethically good way, we conceive of their agency in terms that are not properly determined by who Jesus is and how he is present in them. We see their agency in simple terms as something that belongs to them and is performed by them. We may talk about Jesus as the one *to* whom their obedience is rendered or as the one who models obedience *for* them, but *they* are still the ones who act, whether well or badly. Christ is not personally involved in their obedience; they may be helped or strengthened by the Holy Spirit, but it is they who act. In consequence, when we seek to form them into good moral agents or into better disciples, we think in terms of helping *them* to make better decisions, for which we give *them* credit. Hence, the way we *actually* think about the moral activity or growth of the Christian (what we often label "discipleship") is not really Christ-centered, even if we consider it to be directed toward him. It is, in reality, *self*-centered: we can talk about being "Christlike" or about "relying on the power of the Spirit" but still think about this as something *we* do. When, with the Holy Spirit's help, we are obedient, we are simply better versions of ourselves.

And here lies the problem. Paul's account of the Christian life involves a rejection of the idea that our natural selves can ever be improved or repaired in their own right. They are so compromised by sin that they will only ever turn the gifts of God to the purposes of idolatry and will be blind to the fact that they are doing so, as Paul himself was before his life-transforming encounter with the ascended Christ. People will act, think, teach, and lead in ways that serve this constitutional idolatry and will do so without any self-awareness. Their only prospect for salvation lies in their being inhabited by another self, a better self who can act in them to bring about real goodness. Hence, Paul's personal hope is expressed in his statement "It is no longer I who live, but Christ who lives in me" (Gal. 2:20).[1] This does not mean that his particular distinctive identity has been erased from existence: he still greets the churches to which he writes as "Paul" and still writes in a way that is shaped by his past. But something has changed, and it is not just what his life is directed toward, or how he seeks to live it, but it is his most basic sense of *who* he is, of the person that inhabits the space occupied by his body, of who gets the credit for what his limbs or lips do, of who he is becoming. He is not becoming a better version of Paul; he is becoming Paul-in-Christ. He is metamorphosing[2] into the likeness of Jesus. As difficult as it is for us to comprehend the meaning of such language, a proper understanding of Paul's concept of the Christian moral life demands it.

If the way we think about the Christian life is not adequately shaped by these terms, then here is the danger that awaits: the selves we train to serve God better will be our natural selves, who will only ever embody idolatry, whose attempts to serve will always turn to idolatry, and who—like Paul, like the Pharisees, and like every other religiously diligent self—will labor under the delusion that they are doing splendidly, at least between the episodes of obvious failure that drive them (quite sincerely) to the cross. If a note of anger is detectable under the surface of my words, it is largely directed at myself, for such a way of thinking about the Christian life has undoubtedly marked me over the years and worked itself out in my conduct and

1. I have chosen to quote from the English Standard Version of the Bible (ESV) because I suspect it is the version most widely used by the readers of this book. I will often comment on it or give my own alternative translation. In the latter case, my translation will reflect the difficulty of capturing the overtones of the Greek in idiomatic English; only unidiomatic English—creaky and awkward—will do.

2. This term reflects the Greek word that Paul uses in Rom. 12:2. In Rom. 8:29, he uses a related word, *symmorphos*, to describe our condition of being "conformed" to the likeness of Christ.

values. I was idolatrous in the worst of ways because I thought I was being faithful—in between my moments of undeniable sin. I was an evangelical of evangelicals, of the tribe of Knox; as to zeal, a defender of all evangelical truth claims and an attender of all services; as to doctrine, faultless (in my own mind, at least). Yet over time, I have come to see that the most basic problem I had was the way that I thought about my self: I had not really come to terms with the implications of the gospel for *who* I identified myself to be, although this was a big part of my Reformed theological heritage. This affected all of my piety, all of my relationships, and all of my service.

The process of gradually coming to see this within myself has led me to ask whether the same deficiency might underlie a range of problems affecting the churches today, particularly among those that self-identify as "evangelical."[3] Evangelical churches around the world continue to grow, and many are—in numerical and financial terms, at least—highly successful. It is important not to be cynical about this, but it is also important to be honest in our appraisal of some of the problems that have become visible in many of these churches and to trace carefully their possible causes. In addition to countless stories of controlling and manipulative behavior, especially within leadership, there have been multiple accounts of horrible personal moral failure. You may know the stories that are associated with well-known churches in your part of the world; you may have followed the blog posts about these online, because the congregations have often been seen as evangelical flagships and their pastors as evangelical leaders. I know of such stories that are less well publicized, because the churches in question are smaller and do not register on the national or international radar. It may be that you yourself have been involved

3. This term needs to be used with care. It does not necessarily have the kind of theological significance that we often attach to it. "Evangelical" often functions less as a label for a specific theological account and more as a label for a movement or culture marked by a somewhat fluid set of commitments to specific positions on debates around matters of faith. Many have started to feel uncomfortable with the label, partly in response to perceived problems within "evangelicalism," especially in America and especially in relation to recent political developments. Provided that we are careful to recognize the word's limited significance, though, it remains useful as a term to identify a particular subculture.

in such a story and are still hurting from it. It may be that such an experience awaits you.

These stories should never be allowed to obscure or overshadow the fact that there are countless churches around the world that, while imperfect, embody something genuinely and wonderfully transformative, with leadership that has been genuinely and wonderfully transformed. Part of the task that faces each of us is to ask whether the differences between the churches that are wholesome, if imperfect, and those that appear to be more thoroughly toxic are accidental or systemic. Is it simply that a particular problem has happened to occur in a particular place, with no further explanation required than the pervasiveness of sin in the world, manifesting itself here in this especially visible way? Or is the local problem symptomatic of something systemically wrong with the culture or ideology of the church in question or of its leaders? Might it also be the case that what is wrong is not seen as a problem until its symptoms become dreadfully obvious?

Such questions need to be asked with care if we are not to join the dots wrongly and draw a distorted picture. They need to be asked repeatedly and specifically with such care because we can never draw blanket conclusions; what is true of one situation may not be true of another. They also need to be asked in dialogue with Scripture, as we reflect on its representation of sin as a continuing reality within the church and on its antidote, the gospel of Jesus Christ. My suggestion that the problems may stem from a deficient understanding of our union with Christ may not prove to be correct, or may not be adequate as an explanation, but it must be considered.

Acknowledgments

The core material in this book was delivered as the 2018 Kistemaker Academic Lecture Series at Reformed Theological Seminary in Orlando. I am grateful to Michael Allen and Scott Swain for extending an invitation to give these lectures and for their kind hosting of the event itself. I am also grateful to Ceci Helm and Christina Mansfield for their practical support in relation to my time in Orlando.

The content of the book has been shaped by years of research on the topic of "union with Christ," and my own thinking on the topic has been heavily influenced by interaction with colleagues and with the doctoral students I have supervised. In particular, I would like to thank colleagues at the University of Aberdeen for their (often unwitting) input: Tom Greggs, Paul Nimmo, Phil Ziegler, Ivor Davidson, John Swinton, Brian Brock, and Katy Hockey have all shaped my thinking on these topics in various ways. Several of my doctoral students, current and recent, have also shaped my thinking quite heavily, especially Lisa Igram, Kris Song, Jeannine Hanger, Melissa Tan, and Markus Nikkanen. While all of my students have been invaluable conversation partners, their projects have intersected particularly closely with the content of this one, and they have been a large part of my own research environment.

Within the wider world of New Testament scholarship, several scholars have also been important conversation partners and have been generous with their time and thoughts. John Barclay, Susan Eastman, Simon Gathercole, Matt Novenson, Paul Foster, Elizabeth Shively, David Moffitt, and Tom Wright have probably been the most important voices in the immediate conversation, but a long list of others could be mentioned, some of whom have simply modeled a real depth of Christian kindness.

I am grateful to all involved in the Chalmers Institute in St. Andrews and the group that met to read over the drafts of much of this material; the participants have fed my thinking about its ramifications in all kinds of rich ways. Within that group, Mark Stirling, Jared Michelson, Kenny Robertson, and Dave Redfern deserve special credit for their leadership and vision in bringing this material to bear on the life of the church, especially its leaders.

I am glad to be publishing this particular book with Baker Academic and want to extend my gratitude to the team there. In particular, Dave Nelson provided invaluable feedback on the initial lecture drafts, which contributed to the final shape of the material. I am grateful to have an editor with such theological expertise and wisdom engaging with a work of this kind. Mason Slater and Alex Nieuwsma also deserve to be thanked, in their case for exercising enormous patience with me on the administrative side of things.

Last, a continuing word of thanks to my wife, Jane, and to our church families in the Arbroath Town Mission and Cornerstone St. Andrews and to our network of friends throughout the Free Church. All have continued to provide support, encouragement, and, whenever necessary, challenge. Pete and Joanne Nixon and Kenny and Anna Macleod have been particularly close friends and have helped to model what this book seeks to consider. We are grateful too for the friendship and pastoral oversight of Alasdair and Cathie Macleod over the years. The theme of Alasdair's expository ministry has been simply that "it is all about Jesus," and I can only hope that this is reflected in the pages of the present book.

Abbreviations

General and Bibliographic

alt.	altered
cf.	*confer*, compare
chap(s).	chapter(s)
CSB	Christian Standard Bible
dir.	directed by
diss.	dissertation
e.g.	*exempli gratia*, for example
esp.	especially
etc.	*et cetera*, and so on
Heb.	Hebrew
i.e.	*id est*, that is
lit.	literally
LNTS	Library of New Testament Studies
NIV	New International Version
NT	New Testament
OT	Old Testament
repr.	reprint
SBLDS	Society of Biblical Literature Dissertation Series
SNTSMS	Society for New Testament Studies Monograph Series
trans.	translation, translated by
WUNT	Wissenschaftliche Untersuchungen zum Neuen Testament

Old Testament

Gen.	Genesis	Lev.	Leviticus
Exod.	Exodus	Num.	Numbers

Deut.	Deuteronomy	Isa.	Isaiah
Josh.	Joshua	Jer.	Jeremiah
Judg.	Judges	Lam.	Lamentations
Ruth	Ruth	Ezek.	Ezekiel
1 Sam.	1 Samuel	Dan.	Daniel
2 Sam.	2 Samuel	Hosea	Hosea
1 Kings	1 Kings	Joel	Joel
2 Kings	2 Kings	Amos	Amos
1 Chron.	1 Chronicles	Obad.	Obadiah
2 Chron.	2 Chronicles	Jon.	Jonah
Ezra	Ezra	Mic.	Micah
Neh.	Nehemiah	Nah.	Nahum
Esther	Esther	Hab.	Habakkuk
Job	Job	Zeph.	Zephaniah
Ps(s).	Psalm(s)	Hag.	Haggai
Prov.	Proverbs	Zech.	Zechariah
Eccles.	Ecclesiastes	Mal.	Malachi
Song	Song of Songs		

New Testament

Matt.	Matthew	1 Tim.	1 Timothy
Mark	Mark	2 Tim.	2 Timothy
Luke	Luke	Titus	Titus
John	John	Philem.	Philemon
Acts	Acts	Heb.	Hebrews
Rom.	Romans	James	James
1 Cor.	1 Corinthians	1 Pet.	1 Peter
2 Cor.	2 Corinthians	2 Pet.	2 Peter
Gal.	Galatians	1 John	1 John
Eph.	Ephesians	2 John	2 John
Phil.	Philippians	3 John	3 John
Col.	Colossians	Jude	Jude
1 Thess.	1 Thessalonians	Rev.	Revelation
2 Thess.	2 Thessalonians		

Introduction

Union with Christ as the Basis for Christian Life

Apart from me you can do nothing.

Jesus in John 15:5

There is a Latin expression that is often encountered in popular culture: *sine qua non*. It means "without which nothing." It is an expression we use of something that cannot be omitted or set aside without voiding an endeavor entirely: absent this thing, nothing can be done.

The core claim of this book is that all talk of the Christian moral life must begin and end with Paul's statement "It is no longer I who live, but Christ who lives in me" (Gal. 2:20), and must understand the work of the Holy Spirit rightly in relation to Christ's presence. This assertion is the *sine qua non* of the Christian moral life, which is rendered void in its absence. This means that we can never talk about the moral activity of a Christian without always, in the same breath, talking about Jesus, because the goal of our salvation is not that we become morally better versions of ourselves but that we come to inhabit and to manifest *his* moral identity. This Pauline language is mirrored by the words from John's Gospel, quoted at the opening of this chapter, which develop the organic representation of the Christian as a branch of Christ himself, the vine. It ought, then, to be unthinkable that Christian leaders would see their task as training believers to live more effectively for God without constantly leading them back to this point. Similarly, it ought to be unthinkable that preachers could ever see their task as *simply* explaining the passage before them and showing the moral burdens it places on their congregations, without also feeling compelled to point to the one person *in* whom those responsibilities could be met. And yet, much of our teaching does precisely this. It seeks to make our people "experts in the Scriptures" so that they will be morally prepared to make the right decisions, but that is all they become: not disciples but scribes.[1]

The key point explored in some detail through the body of this book can here be summarized in terms of the prepositions that govern it. Jesus Christ is not represented simply as the one *through* whom we have forgiveness, or even as the one *by* whom the moral life is exemplified, but as the one *in* whom the life of discipleship takes place. Christ himself is present *in* the life of the disciple as the principal moral agent. We are not simply saved *by* him, nor do we merely follow *after* him—though both of these continue to be true—but we participate *in* him. This is why Paul so frequently specifies that the realities of the Christian life are "in Christ." There is no need here to provide some proof-texts of this, for we can hardly turn a page in the Pauline writings without encountering that expression or a close equivalent. The Spirit, meanwhile, who is so important to Paul's account of the moral life, is represented not as helping us to fulfill our frustrated potential but as realizing within us the identity of the Son, and he does this because he himself is the Spirit *of* the Son (Gal. 4:6).

Behind this lies an honest recognition of how sin bears upon our natural selves: sin corrupts each of us through and through, bending our perceptions and values at every level, to the extent that we can only be delivered by someone outside ourselves. This is why we need an "alien" righteousness, for there is no native potentiality for righteousness within us that can meet the need. We need an

---

1. The word "scribes" is used for the experts in the law with whom Jesus clashes in the Gospels. Some versions (e.g., ESV) translate the underlying Greek term simply as "scribes," while others (e.g., NIV) use the more dynamic "teachers of the law."

alien righteousness to be credited to us if we are to stand justified in God's presence, but we also need it to inhabit our limbs, lips, and neurons if we are to live and think in a way that honors God, if we are to confess him rightly. Hence, the plight of the sinner[2] can never be solved *by* the sinner, no matter how well trained or well taught we may be, but only by another: the Righteous One who enters our reality to constitute fresh possibilities for our lives. Any attempt to address the plight apart from this One will serve only the idolatrous instincts of the human condition, what Paul calls "the flesh," and this continues to be true of the Christian life at all points, as idolatrous flesh wars with Christ's Spirit.

Recognizing this, John Calvin famously wrote of salvation as involving a *duplex gratia*, a "double grace" of both justification and sanctification (a word that here indicates moral transformation and growth), in which both parts of the *duplex* are constituted by Jesus, not justification only. This is why Calvin considered any neglect of sanctification to "rend Christ asunder."[3] It was not because justification by faith in Christ ought to result automatically in moral change but because moral change is also a function of the person to whom we are united by the Spirit in faith.

The Problem: A Gospel with Missing Notes

Here, though, is our problem. As I note in chapter 2, the account of salvation that typically underpins models of discipleship within the contemporary church, including within contemporary evangelicalism, differs from Paul's conception (and Calvin's) in subtle but highly problematic ways. It runs along the following lines:

> The death of Jesus pays for our sins, takes the punishment that we deserve, and makes it possible for us to be right with God; once we are right with God, we receive the Holy Spirit to give us the ability to raise our moral game and to live in obedience to God's commandments. We still need the gospel of forgiveness, because even in this new life of

2. Note the use of the noun: sin is not just something we do, however frequently, but something constitutive of what we are.
3. See Garcia, *Life in Christ*.

obedience, we continue to fall into sins that need to be paid for, but the transformation of our lives—sanctification—is a different thing, something that comes through the gift of the Spirit.[4]

Some readers may be surprised by any suggestion that this summary of the gospel is open to question; they may already be reaching for biblical passages that will support such an account of salvation. In the past, I would have done so myself. What we need to consider, however, is that the account is problematic because it does not say *enough*. It does not adequately describe in terms of Christ's own personhood the identity of the believer who lives in fellowship with God. It does not sufficiently articulate how the Spirit is to be identified in relation to Jesus Christ. It allows us to talk about the Christian life as something that *we* practice in fellowship with the Spirit, without really forcing us to pay attention to *who we now are* in Christ. In doing so, it allows key elements of the gospel to be assimilated, without our recognizing it, to a modern individualism that will always compromise our Christian growth.

Let me attempt an extended analogy that I think captures something of the current state of evangelical culture and its account of the gospel. When I was a child, we moved frequently because of my father's work, dragging a piano with us on each of the moves. Over time, that poor piano lost some of its workings: some strings went irremediably out of tune, some hammers became dislodged, and some keys became unusable. That did not stop me from annoying my piano teacher by spending most of my time working out how to play the sound tracks to my favorite movies rather than practicing whatever miserable piece of classical music I was supposed to be learning. Yet I had to work around those missing notes. Major themes became curiously minor as flats were substituted for their letter equivalents; other notes were replaced with ones an octave out of register. As the piano deteriorated further and the number of available notes shrank, the tunes became less and less recognizable, until finally reaching the point that they could no longer be labeled with their original titles. What I was playing could no longer meaningfully be called

---

4. See chap. 2, "Who Am I Really?"

the *Star Wars* theme, for example, because too many of the original notes were missing, and no matter how hard I hit the B-flat, it could not replace the C-sharp. If we had maintained the piano in better condition and ensured that all the notes remained operational, the results would have been fine, but once the notes started to fail, the possibility of playing the tune properly began to be lost. Eventually, I gave up playing altogether, for the piano had really ceased to be a piano and had become an ornament.

The relevant part of this analogy is not the cause of the piano's disrepair but simply its progressively eroding condition. As vital notes from the scale were lost, the remaining notes, though good, were insufficient to make up for their absence. For various historical reasons—good reasons, at that—evangelicals from diverse backgrounds have committed themselves collectively to defending certain truths in the face of their critics. But while we have maintained these notes carefully and have sounded them loudly, gaining a sense along the way of what we hold in common that is distinctively "evangelical," we have allowed other truths to fall into silence. Our ability to sound those other notes where appropriate has been lost. At some point, we must ask ourselves whether we are still playing the original tune or are, perhaps without recognizing it, playing something else, something different. Have we sounded certain good notes so loudly and exclusively that they have come to constitute a different melody? Have we lost so much from our theological scales that what we proclaim is, in fact, a different gospel, much as Paul speaks of something as a "different gospel" in Gal. 1:6? I don't think there is a simple answer to this last question, but the question itself exposes the problem that we need to consider.

Eccentric Participation: Living in Christ and Not in Ourselves

The idea of the Christian self as constituted by Jesus may be difficult for us to wrap our heads around for at least two reasons, both of which I think have contributed to the deterioration of modern accounts of discipleship and ethics. The first is that, as moderns, we are accustomed to speaking about a "person" or a "self" as if it were a thing in its own right, something that can be isolated from the world around it and still have a definable or describable identity. This is the concept that Charles Taylor famously labels "the buffered self,"[5] and it is a very important—and notoriously problematic—feature of modern thought. It underpins much ethical debate, as, for example, in the discussion around whether, or at what stage, rights can be assigned to a fetus or embryo; often this is approached as something connected to the point at which we can meaningfully speak of the embryo attaining personhood. The danger for us is that such a way of thinking about the self—as a buffered, isolable thing that inheres in my body and brain—can be so ingrained that we unwittingly assimilate NT teaching to it. Without thinking, we modify the significance of language that speaks of the self or the person in different ways in order to accommodate this modern concept.[6] We attenuate the force of anything suggesting that "I" might be constituted as a person through my relationships with others, including this particularly significant other called Jesus. This is one of the reasons we find it difficult to comprehend what it means to say "Christ lives in me" or "to live is Christ": each of us assumes that we are an identity in our own right. We lack a category for our identity being formed through our relational encounter with another.

The second reason is more theologically raw. It bears on our identities as something formed not only by our relationships in general but by our relationship with this one particular person, Jesus Christ. Our minds balk at the idea of our selves being constituted in union with Christ because our minds are sinful, and sin seeks to maintain its grip on us even when its power has formally been broken. If sin is, as Luther described it, a turning inward into ourselves,[7] then it

---

5. See Taylor, *Secular Age*. The expression occurs throughout, but important discussions are found on pages 37–42 and 134–42. The latter, in particular, considers the significance of Descartes and the *cogito* for the modern problem of selfhood. For a more comprehensive study of identity, see Taylor's *Sources of the Self*.

6. For a fuller examination of the modern problem and its bearing on the reading of Paul, see Eastman, *Paul and the Person*. Eastman engages broadly and constructively across the modern disciplines that have grappled with how selfhood is to be understood, drawing on philosophy and psychology as well as on theology.

7. The famous expression used by Luther, who lifted the concept from Augustine and applied it to his reading of Paul, is *homo incurvatus in se*. Some modern theology

is entirely opposed to the act of opening ourselves to the indwelling presence of another, particularly *this* other, who has such power to transform us. Sin seeks to dig in, to hold on to what it occupies.

As Susan Eastman has recently pointed out,[8] the language that Paul uses of sin's controlling power (esp. in Rom. 7:20) has some quite striking parallels to the language he uses of Christ's liberating presence (esp. in Gal. 2:20): both are represented with the language of occupation. Sin dwells in us, compromising our agency and controlling our passions: it is no longer I who act, but the sin that dwells in me (Rom. 7:17). The only solution is to be indwelled by a better presence so that we can say, "It is no longer I who live, but Christ who lives in me" (Gal. 2:20). But the sin that inhabits our flesh and our minds will always war with the Spirit, by whom this better indwelling is realized and by whom our minds are transformed. And sin will often do so subtly, disguising its real character with a cloak of religion and piety.

This leads me to a claim that some might find surprising or even offensive. Although we throw the word "sin" around easily and often, especially within evangelicalism, we do not take seriously enough the extent to which it will afflict and subvert our piety—both our practice and our doctrine—if it is not *always* challenged by the gospel. This, surely, is one of the dominant themes of Scripture in both the OT and NT: those who have received the Word of God turn even it toward the ends of idolatry, and they need to be graciously delivered from their corruptions. It was true of those who danced around a golden calf after they had been led out of Egypt (Exod. 32); it was true of the Pharisees (Matt. 23); it was true of the circumcision group in Galatia and the pseudo-humble in Colossae (Col. 2:23). Most unnervingly, it was true of Peter, a Spirit-filled apostle who had to be challenged by Paul (Gal. 2:11–14). In most of these cases, the persons' commitment to Scripture is not in question: no one would claim that the Pharisees did not take God's Word seriously or that Peter's "evangelicalism" was doubtful. But at some point to which they themselves were blind, their piety was warped by sin and began to serve the wrong ends.

---

has been critical of this way of thinking about sin, seeing it as highly androcentric. See Jensen, *Gravity of Sin*.

8. Eastman, *Paul and the Person*, 6–8.

If it was true of them, could it be true of us? Might we, even while congratulating ourselves on our commitments to Scripture and its truths, be thinking in fundamentally idolatrous ways?

Legalism: The Idolatrous Self and the Divine Commandments

We often think of idolatry in terms of putting something in the place that should properly be occupied by God alone. That is not wrong, but it needs to be taken a step further. Idolatry is defined by its subjects as much as it is by its objects; we are constitutionally idolatrous, and that is why we turn things into idols. We put such things in the place that God should occupy because it suits our self-centeredness to do so, even if the things we so place then come to enslave and tyrannize us. We put physical idols that represent gods in that place because we see them as things that can be controlled by us: we can appease them, satisfy them, and manipulate them through our rituals, our worship, and our offerings. If we give them the right things, they will give us rain or sunshine or the right kind of children. Yahweh is not like that, but "the gods" are. When we approach God, we do so on *his* terms; when we approach our idols, we do so on *our* terms, since they are really the things *we* have made to be set in God's rightful place. When those idols then enslave us, it is really our selves that hold us prisoner, because those selves are the things in which sin dwells.

When we put other things in that place (sex, money, success, status, etc.), the same problem is at work: the self is idolatrous because it is self-centered and not God-centered, and having idols of all kinds is the easy way to satisfy the cravings of the self, until the cravings grow worse and the idols grow less rewarding. The easy route to gratification has led us to being owned by the very things we thought would serve our desires.

As I will discuss in chapter 3, Paul uses the same imagery for being enslaved to sin in idolatry—being controlled by the "elemental principles"—that he also uses for legalism. For in truth, legalism is a particular species of idolatry that reflects this same dynamic of self-centeredness. Legalism takes God's good gifts of Scripture and commandments and turns them to the ends of the self, using them as the means to gain symbolic capital by controlling the way others think about us and attempting to control the way God thinks about us.

We need to challenge ways of thinking about legalism that see it as someone else's problem. We tend to think of legalism in terms of a card-carrying commitment to salvation by works, a belief that we ascribe to other religions or to other Christian traditions but from which we ourselves have been delivered. Quite aside from the questions that have been raised about whether the Jews of Jesus's day ever held to such a belief,[9] this way of speaking about legalism does little justice to what seems to be a dominant theme in Galatians: legalism involves pursuing status in the eyes of fellow believers, whether consciously or not, and not just seeking to gain credit before God.

Alternatively, we sometimes think of legalism as if it were identical to the maintenance of traditional values, seeing it as a problem that afflicts older Christians who seem to be more morally constrained than we are. We believe that there is not enough grace in their lives, which is why they are so concerned to follow certain traditional practices. Again, aside from the possibility that we may be judging people whose apparently traditional commitments are actually real manifestations of godly decisions, there is a danger that we overlook our own moral motivations, the drive behind our own practices of prayer or worship. In living out our "vibrant," "modern," "radical" Christianity, are we actually living out the old problem of idolatry, by which even the goodness of God's commands is turned into something that the sinful self can commodify?

Here is the most uncomfortable of thoughts. At a certain point, Paul considers the teaching or beliefs of people who appear to have trusted in Christ and to have received the Spirit to constitute a "different gospel" (Gal. 1:6). Paul labels some such people "false brothers" (2:4), but he also speaks of opposing a fellow apostle (Cephas, i.e., Peter, in 2:11) for acquiescing to such beliefs, and of course he writes to the Galatians because such theology is now rife in their midst.

---

9. These questions were asked carefully in Sanders, *Paul and Palestinian Judaism.* While Sanders's interpretation of Paul has been criticized over the decades, his core claim that grace was a ubiquitous concept in Second Temple Judaism has been broadly accepted, and this in turn has problematized common ways of conceptualizing "works righteousness."

Scripture itself, then, represents this as a corruption that manifests itself within churches that have professed faith in Christ and have experienced the Spirit. It is not a problem that we can simply project onto other traditions of the church without asking first whether it lives among us.

As we will see in chapter 4, the language that Paul uses of this different gospel represents it as a species of the idolatry from which believers are supposed to have been delivered. This, I think, is a particularly stark example of something that runs as a theme throughout the NT: our constitutional sinfulness, our "flesh," will continue to manifest itself in idolatry whenever it is not seen for what it is and treated with its only antidote, the personal presence of Jesus Christ acting through his Spirit. If we begin to think or to speak about any part of Christian life and ethics apart from Christ, our flesh will turn it into idolatry. Even the best of things, even the commandments of God, taken in isolation from Jesus, will become the stuff of idolatry, as they did for the Galatians, because the commandments are easier to deal with than God himself. If we really take sin seriously, we will recognize this; but perhaps our problem is precisely that we don't take sin seriously enough. For all the frequency with which we talk about sin, we don't acknowledge how deeply it compromises us and how absolute our need for Jesus will always be. We are, by nature, idolaters; the only thing that can overcome this reality, whenever it surfaces, is the gospel of Jesus Christ. Each of us must reflect on this: does the label "evangel" in our particular evangelicalism actually designate that different *euangelion* (gospel) of which Paul speaks? Wouldn't that be an awful thing for any of us to admit?

The Present Study: Its Goals and Shape

What I seek to do in the present study is not to provide a comprehensive account of Christian identity or a systematic discussion of Christian philosophies of selfhood. For those interested in such discussions, other studies are available that do a much better job than I ever could.[10] Neither do I seek to give a systematic or comprehensive

---

10. See, e.g., Rosner, *Known by God.*

account of sanctification; again, other excellent studies of this kind are available.[11] Instead, what I will do is work through a number of passages in which Paul's underlying sense of the reconstitution of Christian identity comes through in the warp and woof of his writing. I will draw out how Paul's different way of thinking about identity in Christ disrupts natural ways of thinking about the moral life. This can, in turn, be brought into dialogue with the more systematic studies noted above, helping to qualify or nuance them. More important, it can be brought into dialogue with the thought, speech, and practice visible in the church today.

This identifies the present work as one of practical theology, though it is a particular species of this. It is the kind of practical theology that is shaped quite immediately by engagement with biblical texts, but in ways oriented toward contemporary challenges and questions; it is practical theological interpretation. This is the kind of interpretation that Luther, Calvin, and the other fathers of Protestant theology engaged in. Luther's reading of Paul has often been criticized for projecting his contemporary situation back onto the apostle's writing, but in truth it is a careful reflection on how Paul's teaching speaks into Luther's situation. Whereas modern biblical scholarship is generally satisfied with the findings of exegesis as a historical task (i.e., what Paul meant, what he intended to say), the practical theological task considers how these findings might be related to the contemporary situation (what Paul now means). This involves an awareness of the character of that contemporary situation, elements of which may be novel and alien to that of the ancient situation, and it involves a sensitivity to the fact that no part of Scripture stands alone. Our reading of Paul must be related to the wider canon of Scripture and to the theological traditions. These elements cannot always be visible in what we do, for space is always limited, but they must inform it.

Because the work is oriented toward the task of practical theology, and hence to the life of the church, I have sought to keep footnotes concerning biblical scholarship to a minimum so that they do not clutter the study. In truth, much of the scholarly literature is really

---

11. In particular, I direct readers to Allen, *Sanctification*.

concerned with contextual data, often for its own sake (or for the sake of demonstrating erudition), rather than with data genuinely necessary for interpreting the passage. Where I do cite biblical research, it is because I think it is genuinely relevant not just to biblical scholarship but also to pastoral readings of the biblical material. Also, because of this orientation, I have transliterated the Greek so that the work is readable for those whose training may not have included the biblical languages.

The core of this book (chaps. 2–6) was originally delivered as the 2018 Kistemaker Academic Lecture Series in New Testament at Reformed Theological Seminary in Orlando. My series title was "The Reformed Self in Paul," a play on the theme of personal transformation and the way this theme has been understood in relation to union with Christ in the Reformed tradition. In developing these lectures for publication, it has seemed important to add some further material to contextualize and then conclude my studies. Chapter 1 provides a critical overview of some recent developments in scholarship on Paul and his ethics. Some criticisms will be leveled at other scholarly accounts within this chapter, but for the most part I will simply highlight what I consider to be inadequacies that will be demonstrated by my own readings in the later chapters. Some readers may want simply to skip chapter 1, since the material that follows can be read without it. My sense, though, is that the book would be incomplete without it, since these scholarly movements are quite influential and their effects are felt even at a popular level. Because this chapter will frame what follows in relation to scholarship, it will be fairly heavily footnoted, unlike the remainder of the book. In chapter 2, we will consider what Paul says in the opening chapters of Galatians, relating this to the way he now evaluates his old, natural way of thinking about his righteousness in Phil. 3. Now that the viciousness of his natural self, his flesh, has become visible to him, he has come to recognize that he had been treating righteousness like a commodity that he could own and accumulate, thereby acquiring power over others and over God. Now that he is "in Christ," his whole way of relating to God and the world has changed, and with it his whole way of conceiving righteousness. In chapter 3, we will focus on baptism as a practice that is represented in terms of our union with Christ, which is rendered through the imagery of clothing ourselves with him. In chapter 4, we will look at the role that the Lord's Supper (Eucharist) plays in Paul's account of Christian moral identity: in the Lord's Supper, we occupy and perform a memory of Jesus that makes his story ours and, in doing so, redefines our relationships with the world and with God. In chapter 5, we will consider how sanctification and transformation are portrayed as a genuine struggle, the war of flesh and Spirit, showing how this is represented not in terms of programmatic development but in the personal terms of clothing ourselves with who Christ is. Chapter 6 will then take this imagery of struggle and conflict and relate it to Christian hope, our orientation toward a future that will involve a decisive transformation. Chapter 7 will offer a set of concluding reflections directed explicitly toward pastoral application.

1

Scholarly Contexts
for the Present Study

*Attempts to Revise Our Understanding
of Justification and Sanctification*

This chapter will outline some of the academic debates about Paul's gospel that bear on the topic of this book. As I noted in the introduction, those readers who have no interest in those debates or feel overwhelmed by the technical scholarship they involve may want to skip this chapter and move straight to chapter 2, where my own reading of Paul begins. Although what is discussed here is not essential as background to the later chapters, I think it is important to include it for two reasons. First, some readers will undoubtedly encounter these debates in the context of their own academic development as they are exposed to critical scholarship on Paul, so it will be helpful to position my own reading with respect to this larger field. Second, elements of these debates have filtered down into more popular discussions, particularly within evangelicalism, where ideas are often transmitted without awareness of their academic origins or of the scholarly criticisms that have subsequently been leveled against them. Where the ideas in question involve significant revision of the gospel, as traditionally understood, that can be highly problematic for the life of the church. In some cases, evangelical scholars, including scholarly pastors, have recognized these revisionist accounts of Paul's gospel to be problematic and have openly argued against them. In other cases, evangelicals appear to have embraced the revisions, perceiving them to be important correctives to the deficiencies of their tradition, the diminutions of which I spoke in the introduction. As will be clear from my own discussion, I am less persuaded that the revisionist accounts are satisfactory, though in each case there are elements that are important to affirm.

One common element to many of these revisions is the conviction that Luther's reading of Paul—centered on the concept of justification by faith—has distorted the interpretation not just of the apostle but of the whole NT throughout the modern period. Luther's reading is dismissed as an exercise in unconscious projection or transference of his own situation and his own "hang-ups" back onto Paul's writings.[1] When Paul is read with more historical care against the background of Second Temple Judaism, it is claimed, or when we think more rigorously about the theology of divine grace, then the justification-by-faith model—at least, as traditionally understood—appears foreign to Paul's own thought. Several eminent NT scholars have recently defended Luther's reading and with it much that is considered vital to Protestant theology,[2] but those accusations against the Reformers continue to be sounded, and their validity is largely assumed by biblical scholars.

This issue is important to the task of the present book because the revisionist approaches to Paul affect how we think about the Christian moral life. The issue can be put like this: the revisionists claim that our way of thinking about justification has to be altered to fit Paul's representation of the transformed Christian life; my claim is that our way of thinking about the transformed Christian life has to be altered to make it consistent with Paul's representation of justification. The

1. This is, in part, the thesis of Stendahl, "Apostle Paul and the Introspective Conscience of the West." It has been widely influential in some circles of Pauline scholarship.

2. Notably, John M. G. Barclay, Stephen Westerholm, and Stephen Chester. See below for further details.

key is that both justification and transformation are constituted by our union with Jesus Christ by his Spirit. Those who have defended Luther against his accusers have recognized this coherence to be at work in his thought, though there are elements in Paul's writing that, in my view, they continue to pass over too quickly.

The New Perspective on Paul

The first of the movements that we need to consider is the "New Perspective" on Paul, which is often traced back to the publication of E. P. Sanders's *Paul and Palestinian Judaism.* Sanders challenged the assumption that Jews of the Second Temple period were, if you like, card-carrying legalists who explicitly taught that one is saved by meticulously keeping the law. Carefully examining writings from the Second Temple period and the traditions preserved in the later rabbinic collections, Sanders argued that Judaism could be broadly characterized by the label "covenantal nomism": God establishes his covenant graciously with sinners, and once they are members of the covenant, their lives are regulated by the law, including its multiple provisions for what is to be done when sins continue to be committed. The language famously associated with covenantal nomism is that one "gets in" by grace but "stays in" by observing the law, though the law itself accommodates imperfection and sin. Paul's criticism of those who pursue righteousness by performing "works of the law" cannot then be understood as a simple criticism of people who believed they would be saved by careful adherence to God's commandments rather than by grace. It must instead have a more specific or nuanced meaning, understood only with reference to Paul's new emphasis on participation in Christ, on being "in Christ." What this new way of thinking about participation involved was famously (and with admirable honesty) underdeveloped by Sanders: "But what does this mean? How are we to understand it? We seem to lack a category of 'reality'—real participation in Christ, real possession of the Spirit—which lies between naïve cosmological speculation and belief in magical transference on one hand and a revised self-understanding on the other. I must confess that I do not have a new category of perception to propose here. That does not mean, however, that Paul did not have one."[3] My own previous study, *Union with Christ in the New Testament*, took this as something of a launching point, exploring the ways that this participation in Christ is represented throughout the NT. Here we can simply note that Sanders recognized some of its key elements—the place of the Spirit and the revising of self-understanding—without really knowing what to do with them. Ironically, I think he might have found explanatory categories if he had spent some time reading Luther or the other Reformers.[4]

Sanders's core claim that grace was a ubiquitous concept in Second Temple Judaism has been broadly accepted, even if often qualified.[5] But his interpretation of Paul has been criticized over the decades, particularly his claim that Paul maintained an expectation of a final judgment that would hold people to account for their own works. This is really an outworking of his model of covenantal nomism: one "gets in" by grace but "stays in" by obedience. While Paul has redefined the covenant with respect to Jesus, this basic mode of covenantal operation as something that involves an obedience judged by God still continues. This, I think, is precisely the point where the acknowledged inadequacies of Sanders's attempt to understand "participation" become visible, and my discussion of Paul within this book will illustrate some of the weaknesses. Interestingly, though, it is possible to see partial analogues to Sanders's problematic understanding of Paul in popular contemporary ways of thinking about discipleship, in which the cross is viewed as the gracious entry point into salvation and the gracious means to deal with subsequent sin, but the believer is really responsible for obeying thereafter, even if helped by the Spirit. We "get in" by the cross, but we "stay in" by obedience, even if we need to return to the cross whenever we fail, much as a meticulous law-keeping Jew would have offered a sacrifice. At key points in this book, I will use

---

3. Sanders, *Paul and Palestinian Judaism*, 522–23.
4. Chester, *Reading Paul with the Reformers*.
5. See Carson, O'Brien, and Seifrid, *Justification and Variegated Nomism*; Gathercole, *Where Is Boasting?* John M. G. Barclay (*Paul and the Gift*, 565) makes the crucial observation that "grace is everywhere in the theology of Second Temple Judaism, but not everywhere the same." The conclusion reflects his careful analysis of grace/gift imagery in the ancient world and in Paul.

the New Perspective language to highlight this particular irony in contemporary evangelical thought.[6]

At roughly the same time as Sanders, and in dialogue with his work and with the emerging publications of the Dead Sea Scrolls, N. T. Wright and James Dunn developed similar rereadings of Paul. Wright's has probably been the more influential account, reflecting his admirable commitment to writing extensively for the church and not just for the academy.

Wright, with good warrant, has repeatedly urged readers to recognize that the New Perspective on Paul is really a family of approaches, with each representative developing their account in quite distinctive ways.[7] His own account is particularly attentive to the social or horizontal quality of Paul's rhetoric about works: performance of the "works of the law" appears to be as much about pleasing other people as it is about pleasing God. Comparing Paul to other ancient Jewish literature where similar language is found, notably one of the Dead Sea Scrolls that involves inner-Jewish polemical discussion,[8] he argues that the "works of the law" are actually boundary-maintaining practices that distinguish "insiders" to the covenant from "outsiders." They are practices that visibly set covenant members apart from outsiders, which is why they are physical or public in character (circumcision, Sabbath observance, ritual washing, etc.). Now that the covenant has been redefined in relation to Jesus, the boundaries are to be viewed differently, as indeed they always should have been, since the covenant was always intended to bring about blessing for the whole world.

6. I credit the recognition of this irony to Mark Stirling, my former doctoral student, who now plays a leadership role within evangelicalism in Scotland. He describes an event at which he deliberately used the language of "getting in" and "staying in" in a question directed to prominent evangelical leaders in North America and was shocked that they affirmed what was effectively a covenantal nomistic understanding of salvation: once saved, one has to "stay in" salvation by obeying God's commandments.

7. This is reflected in his use of the plural "New Perspectives" in the title of his helpfully accessible article, "New Perspectives on Paul."

8. The text is designated 4QMMT. The prefix 4Q indicates that it was found in Cave 4 at Qumran, and "MMT" is an acronym for *Miqsat Ma'ase ha-Torah*: "some of the works of the Law." While the significance of 4QMMT runs through much of Wright's work, readers will find a good summary in his article "4QMMT and Paul: Justification, 'Works,' and Eschatology."

Justification, then, is not about the imputation of someone else's credit to our account but designates our insider status within the covenant. For Wright, Luther's problem was that he projected his objections to contemporary ecclesial practices (and to the concepts of virtue that lay beneath them) back onto Paul's language of works and thereby misunderstood the real boundary-focused significance of that language. Once that is recognized, Paul's apparently sustained commitment to the idea of a future judgment in which we will be held to account for our works is easier to explain. Now Paul's account of justification does not minimize or deny the importance of good works or obedience; it simply recasts these in relation to Jesus, who now defines what it means to be in the covenant. This is the element that has worried many evangelical scholars, for it would appear to be at odds with classical notions of grace and imputation, but for Wright it is an important element in a moral account that expects the church to serve, actually and effectively, in the world. The community that is bound in covenant union with Christ will work in the world to realize the values of his kingdom and thereby bring blessing. This shapes their distinctive virtue[9] and ties it to the story of Jesus himself that is recounted in the Gospels. Paul's gospel is shaped, not narrowly by his perception of the cross and resurrection described at the end of the Gospel story, but by the whole narrative of Jesus Christ, set within the framework of the story of Israel.[10]

I consider Wright's account, like that of Sanders, to be marked by an inadequate understanding of what it means to participate in Christ, but the problems are quite finely grained and need to be traced carefully; they are not as easily identified as some critics of Wright seem to think. The core problem, in my view, is that Wright does not pay correct attention to the pneumatic (i.e., Spirit-constituted) character of Christian agency and how this relates to Christian selfhood. This is the result of his more basic decisions concerning the rendering of salvation within the biblical story, in turn affected by theological decisions about how one should talk about God and Jesus.

9. For this dimension of Wright's thought, see his *Virtue Reborn*, published in the US as *After You Believe*.
10. See now Wright's massive study *Paul and the Faithfulness of God*.

For Wright, Christian participation is covenantal in character (a point with which I agree), but that covenant really formalizes our external relationship with God in relation to Jesus. While Wright takes very seriously the extent to which Christian identity is reconstituted in relation to Jesus—allowing Gal. 2:20 to play a key role in his interpretation of Paul—his description of Christian morality does not, I think, adequately deal with the way that Paul speaks of Jesus acting in and through him and other believers by the Spirit. Instead, it is shaped by the way Wright conceives participation within his controlling model of the biblical story. In commenting on Gal. 2:19–20, for example, he writes, "Paul is not here recounting his own 'religious experience' for the sake of it. He is telling the story of what has happened to Israel, the elect people of God—and he is using the rhetorical form of quasi-autobiography, because he will not tell this story in the third person, as though it were someone else's story, as though he could look on from a distance (or from a height!) and merely describe it with a detached objectivity."[11] This leads Wright to understand participation principally in terms of the *vocation* of God's people within this story, the purpose for which they have been elected. This can have a certain ring of moralism that is reflected in Wright's account of judgment: *we* will still be judged according to what *we* have done. This is one of the reasons why Wright's evangelical critics have considered him to have abandoned a proper account of justification by faith, as he redefines justification in terms of true covenant membership and vocation. The point I make here is that the problem is less a function of Wright's understanding of justification language and has more to do with his neglect of elements in Paul's account of the Christian life that need to be explicated in terms of agency rather than story. For Paul, it is not just that we participate in the story of the Messiah through our sharing of his vocation, but that he is *actually* present in us and working through us in an immediate and personal sense.

11. Wright, *Paul and the Faithfulness of God*, 852. See also his comments on 858: "[Paul] understands this action as drawing to its divinely ordained focal point the entire story of the election of Israel (that is why he can say 'the grace of God' in verse 21, as a further way of referring to what has happened on the cross), and *redefining* it around the Messiah, who has at last offered to the covenant God the 'faithfulness' of Israel" (emphasis original).

In my view, this neglect is actually a function of Wright's avoidance of classical theology and its identifications and categories, particularly those of the classical trinitarian formulations and two-natures Christology. In keeping with most contemporary biblical scholars, he avoids these kinds of categories in his discussion of Paul, seeing them as the product of later Greek philosophical theology, but because of this, his work lacks a conceptual framework found in the fathers (and, for that matter, in Luther) that would allow him to speak of how the Spirit works to actualize the presence of the Son within us. The best way I can defend this claim is simply by seeking, in my own discussion throughout this book, to highlight the ways in which such elements help us to make sense of the details of Paul's writing. Even if not yet developed into the categories later offered by the fathers, Paul's soteriology takes seriously both the divine and the human natures of Jesus (without dissolving that word "divine" into a label merely for function) and the distinctive identity of the Spirit. It is important to note, though, that Wright's under-reading of such elements in Paul is arguably paralleled in his reading of Luther. Wright's representation of Luther suggests that the Reformer's problem was his view of the law and how it relates to justification, but that theme is really subsidiary in Luther to his view of the self. At the heart of Luther's objection to medieval Catholic accounts of virtue is a recognition that the self—including *his* self—is desperately and deceitfully sinful and can be delivered only by a savior outside of that self.[12] This was not a mistakenly individualistic reading of Galatians fed by Luther's personal sense of guilt, among other factors, but a serious reading of the language about personal agency in Galatians, read honestly by someone willing to hold up that light to himself and his peers.

Some recent scholarship has more thoroughly considered the inadequacy of the New Perspective reading of Luther. Rather than seeing Luther as projecting his own context and concerns onto Paul, violating the original sense of Paul's thought, they have recognized that Luther read Paul carefully and then—with equal care—considered how the apostle's teaching could be brought to bear on his contemporary

---

12. For some of the differences between Paul and his peers or predecessors in thinking about virtue, see Herdt, *Putting on Virtue*, 173–96.

situation.[13] Elements of the New Perspective certainly continue to be persuasive to most biblical scholars, notably the recognition that Jews widely and frequently understood their salvation in terms of grace and cannot be considered "legalistic" in simplistic terms, but there is a growing recognition that the "Lutheran" views it rejects are really the popular versions found in traditions that can trace their lineage back to the Reformation—that is, Protestant and evangelical churches. In other words, the proponents of the New Perspective rightly reacted to the distortion of the gospel (and the nature of its opposition to "works") detectable in much Protestant and evangelical interpretation of Paul, but they were wrong to trace this back to Luther. It is comparable to someone who hears an attempt to play Beethoven on a dilapidated piano and dismisses the composer's original works as "jarring."

If we take Luther's reading of Paul seriously again—while recognizing that it is driven not by an evaluation of the law but by an evaluation of the self as something deluded into believing that it is intrinsically capable of acquiring symbolic capital through its own activities—then we can grasp more readily how the social and religious aspects of works (the vertical and the horizontal, if you like) proceed in codependence from this basic distortion of one's sense of identity. Once I grasp that *I* am incompetent to do any kind of good, I begin to open myself to the need for someone else to help me, which is the recognition that lies at the core of Paul's gospel. This recognition will allow us to affirm elements in the New Perspective on Paul, particularly concerning the social dimension of "works of the law," while also pressing back on its critique of classic notions of justification.

The Turn to Virtue in Theology and Pauline Studies

Emphasizing identity and selfhood, and recognizing that Luther was actually attentive to something important in Paul's representation of these, also has implications for the resurgence of interest in

13. Notably Barclay, *Paul and the Gift*. See also Westerholm, *Perspectives Old and New on Paul*.

virtue-based approaches to Paul's ethics specifically and to Christian ethics more broadly. These approaches affirm the importance of moral identity or character and personal formation, in distinction from approaches that focus on the act rather than the agent. Act-centered approaches to ethics consider whether a particular action can justifiably be called good or bad; agent-centered approaches consider how good or bad actions proceed from good or bad persons. Within virtue theories, the moral character of an agent is subject to complex formational processes that involve appetites and instincts, with these becoming well ordered in the virtuous person but remaining disordered in the vicious one. The loss of "virtue" as a category in ethics is typically traced back to the birth of modernity as an intellectual culture that emerged from the closely intertwined Reformation and Enlightenment. Luther criticized the medieval accounts of virtue for what he considered to be an inadequate recognition of the self's corruption and an insufficiently Christocentric understanding of its amelioration; the Enlightenment refocused all ethical discourse onto rationalistic debates about the warrant for particular acts.

The renewal of interest in virtue and character among Protestant scholars has exposed the deficiencies of act-centered approaches that focus almost exclusively on obedience to divine commandments or on the imitation of Jesus. To focus on such activities, without giving deeper consideration to the moral identity of the person who seeks to perform them, is simply superficial. It ignores the fact that much of our life is taken up by activities that are not regulated by divine commandments and that can be performed virtuously or viciously, it ignores the risk of performing a superficial or outward obedience to commandments while having a heart that continues to be selfish, and it ignores the complex of appetites behind our actions and thoughts that need to be addressed as part of our moral growth.[14] The return to virtue in Protestant and evangelical theology has resulted

14. The key work that contributed to the broader resurgence of interest in virtue is MacIntyre, *After Virtue*. Within Protestant theological ethics, Stanley Hauerwas has been more widely influential, notably his *Character and the Christian Life*. More recently, James K. A. Smith has made vibrant contributions to Protestant moral theology that draw upon this approach. See his *Desiring the Kingdom* and *You Are What You Love*.

in a welcome shift in focus toward concepts of formation and their appetitive dimensions.

The broader renewal of interest in virtue theory has had an impact on Pauline scholarship. Some scholars have been freshly attentive to the influence of classical accounts of virtue (notably that of Aristotle) on Paul's thought. They have noted the way Paul speaks of the moral transformation of believers themselves and not just the actions that they perform, and they have seen the technical language of virtue to be at work in his writing.[15] A small number of scholars have claimed that Paul's thought can be located quite close to Stoicism, with its very particular understanding of personal self-regulation and formation.[16]

While this renewed interest in Paul's emphasis on moral identity—as distinct from moral activity—is broadly helpful and indeed is in line with the claims that I make in this book, a counterpoint needs to be established. For however much Paul may use the language of personal transformation and moral identity and however much of this he may draw from the virtue accounts of his day, his way of speaking about the identity of a believer "in Christ" is fundamentally different from anything that we encounter in Greek philosophy.[17] His pessimism concerning the ability of the natural self to be anything other than idolatrous and his identification of the basis for transformation to be found only in Jesus are highly distinctive.[18] As Stanley Hauerwas and Charles Pinches put it: "Jesus of Nazareth is a far cry from Aristotle's magnanimous man."[19]

To repeat this in language that we have already used in this chapter: virtue theory is concerned with how we can become better versions

---

15. See, e.g., Wright, *Virtue Reborn*, published in the US as *After You Believe*.

16. Notably, Troels Engberg-Pedersen in his *Paul and the Stoics* and his later *Cosmology and the Self in the Apostle Paul*.

17. For a very technical discussion of how this is reflected in Paul's vocabulary, see Frederick, *Ethics of the Enactment and Reception of Cruciform Love*.

18. One study that seeks to take this seriously, while still reading Paul in terms of virtue, is Miller, *Practice of the Body of Christ*. I am not persuaded that Miller's study deals adequately with the distinctive personhood of Son and Spirit in relation to the identity of the believer, but it is a welcome attempt to read the apocalyptic Paul in relation to virtue ethics.

19. Hauerwas and Pinches, "Virtue Christianly Considered," 302.

of ourselves as we order our appetites and instincts, but Paul is concerned with how we become someone else. That point needs to be maintained carefully in all conversation about virtue and personal formation. There was a reason why Luther considered the virtue accounts of his day to be incompatible with Paul's gospel.

The Apocalyptic Paul, the Perfection of Grace, and the Faith of Jesus Christ

The New Perspective and virtue-based readings of Paul pay inadequate attention to the decisive role that Christ's moral identity plays in the apostle's understanding of Christian sanctification. At this point, I have only made this claim, but in the course of chapters 2–6, my reading of Paul will defend it. A different strand of NT scholarship takes the decisive significance of Christ's identity seriously— again in reaction to the perceived deficiency of traditional accounts of justification by faith—but does so in ways that are also problematic, both as an interpretation of the apostle and as a foundation for Christian ethics. The works that I have in mind typically place a healthy emphasis on both the importance of Christology for Paul's account of salvation and the absolute centrality of divine grace, rightly asserting that the work of Christ in our behalf is entirely and solely the grounds of our salvation. But they move from this to a way of speaking of the Christian life that suggests both our practicing of faith and our *experience* of moral development are simply immaterial to salvation. This proceeds from a particular way of thinking about grace that is heavily shaped by theological reflection, and the scholarship in question often sees itself as more theologically sensitive than most biblical scholarship.[20]

The works in question represent a particular subgrouping within what is often labeled the "apocalyptic Paul" school. This label probably suggests more consistency than actually exists among the accounts offered by the various scholars associated with this group. In

20. For the self-consciously theological aspect of this approach, see Davis and Harink, *Apocalyptic and the Future of Theology*; and Tilling, *Beyond Old and New Perspectives on Paul*.

truth, while they share certain traceable lines of influence, they are only loosely associated by their common conviction that Paul's gospel is principally defined in terms of deliverance from the powers of sin and death, with guilt and forgiveness operating within this schema rather than being the totality of the gospel. Typically, they understand the gospel as involving some kind of participation in Christ's victory over these powers and tend to see that victory as an invasive reality that has broken into the present evil age. The label "apocalyptic" has little to do with the genre of ancient literature that shares that appellation and is, instead, linked to Paul's language of the gospel being "revealed" (or "apocalypsed") to him, as in Gal. 1:16. This revelation transformed how Paul evaluates his past life, which he now sees was wrapped up in this world that is ruled by the powers of sin and death, from which he has been delivered. It is this new set of perceptions that lies behind Paul's negative account of the law; his gospel is not the next stage in the development of God's relationship with Israel but breaks into the world as something radically new. The approach is usually traced back through J. Louis Martyn, especially his commentary on Galatians, to Ernst Käsemann's "Beginnings of Christian Theology" and his influential commentary on Romans.[21]

While the details of this approach can be interrogated, particularly related to Paul's view of the Torah or to the genre "apocalypse," the apocalyptic reading of Paul is generally helpful in calling attention to the cosmic qualities of Paul's gospel. It recognizes the participatory character of his account of salvation and takes seriously the disruptive implications of his language. More than anything, it highlights that Paul's concept of salvation is never only about forgiveness and status but is unavoidably about deliverance from the power of sin. It recognizes that neither sin nor its solution can ever be naturalized, as if they are just negative patterns of behavior to be corrected and forgiven and replaced with their sanctified equivalents; they can only ever be represented using the language of powers that are overthrown by the victory of Jesus.[22]

21. Martyn, *Galatians*; Käsemann, "Beginnings of Christian Theology," translated from "Die Anfänge christlicher Theologie"; Käsemann, *Commentary on Romans*.
22. For a superb exploration of the theological value of the apocalyptic approach to Paul, see Ziegler, *Militant Grace*.

For our purposes, one of the most valuable developments of the apocalyptic approach has been a renewed interest in the nature of divine agency and how this relates to human agency in the context of a world that is perceived to be saturated with powers. A number of studies have emerged that consider in detail the evidence from the ancient world concerning perceptions of divine and human agency,[23] and some have brought this to bear on the major movements in modern scholarship and the assumptions that they often make concerning this.[24] Perhaps the most valuable of these works, and the one most closely aligned with the purposes of the present study, is Susan Eastman's *Paul and the Person*, which we mentioned in the introduction. Eastman distinctively frames the question of divine and human agency in terms of personhood and identity, drawing on modern philosophy and scientific research along the way. This moves beyond the general interest in divine and human agency, which tends to focus on *how* they relate or even on *where* they relate (i.e., in the context of a world that is influenced by the presence of good and evil powers), and considers *who* we are as moral agents associated with the presence of Christ. The principal difference between her work and the present one is not a matter of conclusions but rather of the range of Pauline texts that are studied and the detail that emerges in the process.

While the apocalyptic approach is broadly helpful, a subcategory within it moves beyond the elements outlined above to something that redefines the most basic terms of faith. In the case of Douglas A. Campbell, who is probably its most influential exemplar,[25] the account involves a logical distinction between alleged conditional (or "contractual") ways of thinking about salvation and unconditional ones, with the latter held to be more consistently governed by the concept of grace.[26] The classical "Lutheran" way of thinking about

23. See, e.g., Barclay and Gathercole, *Divine and Human Agency*.
24. Croasmun (*Emergence of Sin*), e.g., engages closely with Bultmann's view of human agency, which is wrapped up in the existentialist framework of his thought.
25. Notably in Campbell's *Deliverance of God*.
26. This is developed throughout Campbell's massive study, *Deliverance of God*, but particularly important discussions are found on pages 64–65 and 100–105. For an excellent overview and analysis of Campbell's argument, see Barclay, *Paul and the Gift*, 171–73.

justification by faith is contractual because it involves a condition: we benefit from justification only if we believe something.[27] Hence, the faith that is crucial to the justification-by-faith model is a kind of work, and the model must therefore be considered inconsistent with a thoroughgoing affirmation of grace. A true affirmation of grace—which Campbell considers to be essential to Paul's gospel—will prevent any way of thinking about salvation that makes it conditional on a human response, even that of faith.[28] Campbell labels his own account "participatory" and locates the center of Paul's theology in the description of transformation found in Rom. 6–8 (which he defines in terms of "sanctification"), but his way of speaking about divine grace excludes any sense that this transformation must involve any deliberate human response. This has a bearing on the way moral growth is considered: it might happen, but if divine grace really does define our understanding of the gospel, then moral growth cannot be considered an essential element of the Christian life. The logic of grace prevents us from seeing any human response to God as an essential part of salvation.

This of course requires Campbell (and others who follow such an approach) to provide a different explanation of the language of faith (*pistis*) in Paul, one that avoids the problem of considering it a condition of salvation. This explanation is found in the debate around the significance of the expression *pistis Christou* (faith of/in Christ) in Paul. In principle, it is grammatically legitimate to understand this construction in either objective or subjective terms: either Jesus is the object of faith (the one in whom faith is placed or with whom faith is concerned) or he is the active subject of the faith in question (the one who is faithful).[29] Classical theology (not just justification theory) has held to the former view—that Jesus is the object of faith—but Campbell and others see the phrase *pistis Christou* as denoting the faithfulness enacted by Jesus. Hence, when Paul says that we are justified "through [the] faith of Jesus Christ," he is speaking

---

27. The problem of sin is also defined contractually: we are guilty because we have suppressed a rational knowledge of God and have not met our obligations to worship him.

28. A similar point is made in Hays, *Faith of Jesus Christ*.

29. For an overview of the debate, see Bird and Sprinkle, *Faith of Jesus Christ*.

not of our faith in Jesus but of his faithfulness on our behalf. This allows Campbell to consider *pistis* as an act performed by God, in Christ, and hence to be located on the divine side of the relationship between God and humans. It is not a condition of salvation that we must perform but a redemptive action performed already by God; nothing we do can alter its significance.

I consider this problematic for two reasons. First, there is good evidence that the particular syntax employed in the expression "through *pistis Christou*" is best understood in the objective sense. Stanley Porter and Andrew Pitts have highlighted that when a head noun ("faith") occurs without a definite article ("the") but with a controlling preposition ("through") and is qualified by a genitive ("Jesus Christ"/"Christ"),[30] the structure normally is read objectively.[31] This may be difficult for nonspecialists to follow, but basically the fact that Paul uses the expression "through faith of Christ" and not "through *the* faith of Christ" means that it would most naturally be read in Greek to designate Jesus as the object of the faith in question, the one in whom faith is placed.

If the preceding argument is difficult to follow, and certainly only Greek language specialists can judge its merits, the second one is much more straightforward: Paul's use of the vocabulary of faith is hardly confined to this expression or even to the noun *pistis*. We have to interpret his thought in a way that takes into account the range of ways he represents Christians as people who enact "faith" in some way. For example, Rom. 3:22 follows the reference to *pistis Christou* with the plural participle "all *believers*" (*pantas tous pisteuontas*), something that is broadly paralleled in Gal. 3:22. Galatians 2:16, meanwhile, also uses the finite plural verb *episteusamen* (we believed). Plenty of further examples and parallels with other verbs could be identified, but the point can be made simply from those given here: Christians are agents of the verbs of faith, and that is inextricably linked to their justification.

While the decision to adopt a subjective interpretation of *pistis Christou* is problematic, in the view of many scholars, the debate

30. The full title "Jesus Christ" is used in Rom. 3:22; Gal. 2:16; and 3:22, but Gal. 2:16 also repeats the construction using only "Christ."
31. See Porter and Pitts, "Πίστις with a Preposition and Genitive Modifier."

has helped to reassert the importance of Christ's own faith as the basis for the participatory reality of our faith. The key point that will emerge in my own study is that the participatory quality of our faith, which is constituted by someone outside of ourselves, is not at odds with the pivotal significance that Paul attaches to the activity of believing. We might agree with Campbell that the faith of Christians is really a matter of participation in Christ's own faith, with which it is "isomorphic,"[32] but we cannot thereby minimize or negate the importance of our own responsive or receptive[33] faith, as Campbell goes on to do.

The decision to understand the expression *pistis Christou* as speaking of the faithfulness of Jesus often accompanies a reading of Paul that minimizes or even dismisses the significance of Christian growth and moral maturation. This dismissal is the corollary of an exaggerated emphasis on divine grace, which is understood to allow no expectation of reciprocity or return.[34] Logically, this determines not only God's attitude toward the one who has believed but also God's attitude toward everyone and everything. If not, God's attitude toward them would be dependent on their actions, which would occasion his wrath, and we would be back to a way of thinking about God that is not sufficiently determined by the concept of his grace.

This way of thinking about grace would seem to fly in the face of much of Paul's teaching. In Rom. 1–4, Paul appears to frame the problem of sin in terms of an idolatrous failure to obey God, a failure that involves both culpability and corruption, which suggests that God expects us to conform to some kind of moral standard

32. Campbell, *Deliverance of God*, 756.
33. To describe faith as "receptive" is helpful. The language of grace identifies salvation as a gift that originates outside ourselves, in the accomplishment of which we are passive but in the enjoyment of which we are not inert.
34. It is important not to caricature Campbell on this point (although his representation of Reformed concepts of justification by faith is itself something of a caricature). Campbell's whole thesis centers on the concept of participatory transformation, often labeled "sanctification." In a critical exchange with Scott Hafemann, Campbell rejects any notion that his denial of conditional or contractual readings of Paul entails a denial of responsiveness to God's work. He affirms human responses to the gospel while denying that they have any conditional significance for salvation or the enjoyment of God's blessing. See Hafemann, "Reading Paul's ΔΙΚΑΙΟ-Language"; and Campbell, "Douglas Campbell's Response to Scott Hafemann."

that defines justification and sanctification. His verdict on our lives would appear to be conditioned in some sense by our actions. For Campbell, this is simply incompatible with Paul's emphasis on divine grace, and he is forced to find a rather creative way of reconciling the surface detail of the text with the alleged underlying theology. Paul, he claims, here uses a rhetorical practice known as *speech in character*:[35] at those points where Paul seems to frame the gospel in terms that sound inconsistent with the concept of grace (as Campbell understands it), the apostle is actually quoting an ideological opponent whose terms he goes on to reject. Few have been persuaded by this particular suggestion,[36] but Campbell's broader understanding of grace and his rejection of more traditional covenant theology as essentially contractual[37] is proving to be both popular and influential in some evangelical circles.

This reading of Paul is influenced by certain important strands of modern theology, particularly the work of Karl Barth (though typically refracted through the lens of the "Torrance Theology").[38] It is an important and often genuinely insightful body of scholarship on Paul that deserves to be considered seriously and calls attention to the participatory character of Paul's gospel. While its decision to understand the language of *pistis Christou* as a subjective genitive is problematic, it invites us to think in more subtle ways about how even the faith of believers is constituted by the person of Jesus Christ and his relationship to the Father. This is something that I will consider in the following chapters, particularly chapter 6. But as Barclay has

35. The technical word for this is *prosōpopoeia*.

36. See, e.g., my discussion in Macaskill, "Review Article: *The Deliverance of God.*"

37. This view is heavily dependent on J. B. Torrance's analysis of federalism within the Scottish Reformed tradition, "Covenant or Contract." The distinction between covenant and contract and the significance that Torrance attached to it has been heavily criticized. See my own discussion of this in *Union with Christ*, 89–92.

38. For the relationship of apocalyptic theology generally to Barth, see Ziegler, "Some Remarks on Apocalyptic in Modern Christian Theology." Campbell's reading is distinctively shaped by the refraction of Barth in the theology of J. B. Torrance, an influence acknowledged in *Deliverance of God*. The influence of T. F. Torrance, particularly on Campbell's categories of methodological Arianism versus methodological Athanasianism discussed below, is acknowledged in Campbell's article "Current Crisis."

recently highlighted, it assumes a definition of the word "grace" that moves beyond its actual meaning or usage. It is a *Princess Bride* moment: "You keep using that word; I do not think it means what you think it means."[39] Barclay's careful evaluation draws on the concept of "perfection," where an element within a particular concept (here, grace) is either extended beyond its proper significance or isolated from other parts of the concept in a way that results in a kind of caricaturing: "The term 'perfection' . . . refers to the tendency to draw out a concept to its endpoint or extreme, whether for definitional clarity or ideological advantage."[40] This kind of activity looses a word or concept from the constraints that properly control it in speech, thought, or usage. As Barclay indicates with his language of "ideological advantage," this act can often lead to a concept being redefined in ways distinct from its traditional or proper usage. He writes, "One way to legitimate oneself as the bearer of a tradition, and to disqualify others, is to appropriate to oneself the 'true' and 'proper' meaning of a traditional concept, such that others are not simply limited in understanding but are fundamentally in error: what *they* mean by X is non-X, once it has been defined in a particular, 'perfect' form."[41] Barclay then traces various ways in which certain characteristics of grace are "perfected" by particular thinkers, taken to the point of caricature, and often defined in ways that exclude other characteristics. He notes six characteristics in particular that have been perfected in this way: superabundance, singularity, priority, incongruity, efficacy, and non-circularity.[42]

---

39. The line is taken from the movie *The Princess Bride* and is famously delivered by Mandy Patinkin (playing the swordsman Inigo Montoya) in response to the Sicilian's repeated (and inappropriate) use of the word "inconceivable." It has become something of a cultural meme for the inaccurate use of language. The line in the original book is slightly different: "'You keep using that word!' the Spaniard snapped, 'I don't think it means what you think it does.'" Goldman, *Princess Bride*, 102.

40. Barclay, *Paul and the Gift*, 67. Barclay draws this from Burke, *Permanence and Change*, 292–95; and Burke, *Language as Symbolic Action*, 16–20.

41. Barclay, *Paul and the Gift*, 68.

42. Another word for "superabundance" is "extravagance" (Barclay, *Paul and the Gift*, 70). "By 'singularity' I mean that the giver's *sole* and *exclusive* mode of operation is benevolent goodness" (70–71). Barclay describes "priority" as follows: "Here the focus lies on the timing of the gift, which is perfect in taking place always

The discussion of perfections is an important part of Barclay's overall argument, but when he applies it specifically to Campbell, he notes that all of these perfections are at work, though the last most of all. Campbell's definition of grace allows no room for the gift to be given with an expectation on God's part that those who receive it will render something to him in turn. This is in contrast to Barclay's own overarching argument, which sees God as giving the gift of salvation to those who are unworthy of it and incapable of rendering any return but who are transformed by the gift they receive in such a way that they meaningfully respond. Barclay's way of putting this is that the gift is given to the unfitting, but it brings about a "fittingness" in them. Crucially, though, Campbell's perfecting of grace—which actually parallels the ways Marcion perfected the concept[43]—functions in the ideological way that Barclay has described. By perfecting the characteristics of grace in this way, particularly its non-circularity, and claiming that his way of thinking about grace is shared with the fathers of the tradition, notably Athanasius, Campbell can label those with whom he disagrees as fundamentally in error. Those who subscribe to the notion of justification by faith and affirm the importance of the human response to grace in the experience of salvation are functionally Arian, operating

---

prior to the initiative of the recipient" (71). About "incongruity" Barclay says, "It is normally emphasized in antiquity that gifts should be given generously, but selectively; care should be taken that the gift is given to suitable, worthy or appropriate recipients. . . . It is always possible to argue, however, that such a limitation of the gift was less than fully generous; a perfect gift could be figured as one given without condition, that is, *without regard to the worth of the recipient*" (72–73, emphasis original). The characteristic of "efficacy" is included because "a perfect gift may also be figured as that which fully achieves what it was designed to do" (73). "Non-circularity" can also be described as "non-reciprocity": "Is a gift defined as a gift by the fact that it escapes reciprocity, the system of exchange or *quid pro quo* that characterizes sale, reward or loan? As we have seen, such is the modern notion of the 'pure gift.' . . . This was not a common conception of gifts in antiquity. . . . The one-way gift establishes no relation, creates a permanent and potentially humiliating dependency, and frees the recipient of all responsibility. Nonetheless, *its emergence in the modern era as a powerfully alluring perfection of grace, identified with 'pure' altruism or disinterest, makes this an important facet of the perfected gift* to place alongside the others we have outlined" (75, emphasis added).

43. Barclay, *Paul and the Gift*, 173.

with an unexamined foundationalism[44] and a contractual notion of salvation. This includes Luther.[45]

Barclay's analysis of the gift and its capacity to bring about fittingness in those who receive it is an important challenge to Campbell's account and brings us full circle to Luther, whose reading of the gospel is one that Barclay considers to be broadly correct. Luther's reading is not an act of transference or projection of contemporary issues back onto Paul but a careful application of Paul's teaching to his own day and age and to himself. My own contribution will not cover this ground again. Instead, I offer a close reading of some of the passages that speak of our transformation in Christ as entailing a real, if difficult, experience and the practicing of faith as a key element in our participation in Christ's righteousness. We can never repay God in kind for what he has done for us, but our prayers of thanksgiving and our acts of service are not immaterial to him. I offer this reading in the hope that those seeking to correct some problematic emphases in modern notions of discipleship will not replace these with equally problematic alternatives.

The Imitation of Christ: What Would Jesus Do?

One final movement in scholarship is worth mentioning here, much more briefly, as it frames our reading of Paul's moral theology in important ways and resembles some popular ways of thinking about Christian ethics. The scholarship in question focuses on the imitation of Christ as the defining characteristic of Christian morality and is perhaps best represented by the work of Richard

---

44. Campbell identifies this foundationalism in the assumption that he considers to be at work in all justification theory—namely, that everyone can be considered culpable because they have some rational knowledge of God that they have suppressed. This is opposed to the apocalyptic approach, as he advocates it, which sees the knowledge of God as something that comes only by divine self-disclosure, in the apocalypse constituted by the incarnation.

45. See Campbell, *Deliverance of God*, 109–32. See also Campbell, "Current Crisis." Campbell's arguments—including his attempt to map all Pauline scholarship onto the Athanasian-Arian debate—have been heavily criticized, with patristic specialists included among the voices that have considered his claims to be distortive. See, e.g., J. Warren Smith, "'Arian' Foundationalism or 'Athanasian' Apocalypticism."

Burridge.[46] Like many others,[47] Burridge is sensitive to the way that "the gospel" is often reduced to the narrative of Jesus's death and resurrection, loosed from the accounts of his life and ministry. Building on his earlier research into the biographical character of the Gospels,[48] Burridge seeks to show how the NT writers all develop representations of Christian ethics that are shaped by the life and teaching of Jesus, not just by his death and resurrection (though those events remain, of course, pivotal). Because the Gospels are biographies (or *bioi*), they recount the narrative of Jesus's life as an enactment of his identity; Christian ethics are principally about the emulation or imitation of that identity. In his careful analysis of the NT writings, Burridge highlights the range of ways in which the writers point their readers toward the biographical narratives of Jesus as exemplary for Christian life and thought.

There is much to appreciate in Burridge's work. Aside from the extensive analysis of connections and allusions that link NT ethics to the life of Jesus, his work highlights a dominant theme within these: inclusivity. But it suffers from the same problem as the more popular "What Would Jesus Do?" movement: a lack of attentiveness to the way that the NT writers represent Christian moral identity *principally* as inhabitation rather than imitation. As we shall see in this book, it is because we are united to Christ, clothed with Christ, baptized into Christ, and we abide in Christ that we can also meaningfully imitate him. Absent that key element, all we have is moral heroism. In Burridge's case, the images of participation seem to be taken as representations of our dynamic experiences of Christian community: "in Christ" is really just a way of saying "in the church that imitates Christ." This means that inclusive Christian love is represented as the goal or *telos* of our community, something that we work toward; when we experience or manifest this, we will meaningfully imitate the fellowship of God himself. But, as we will also see throughout this book, Paul's representation of Christian unity is that it is actually a matter of participation in the oneness of the God to

46. Burridge, *Imitating Jesus*.
47. A similar concern drives much of N. T. Wright's work, as exemplified by *New Testament and the People of God* and *Jesus and the Victory of God*.
48. Burridge, *What Are the Gospels?*

whom we are united. It is not so much our *telos* as it is our basis. It is not that we are to gradually eradicate disunity and exclusion and thereby come to a better imitation of Jesus; it is that the presence of any disunity is essentially at odds with what we are: in union with the one God through the one mediator.

Those drawn to the "What Would Jesus Do?" approach may be drawn to a work such as Burridge's, and it will certainly make a valuable contribution to their thinking, but the concept of imitation has its limits. There is only so much moral example that can be meaningfully derived from studying the life of Jesus, and many of our moral situations will simply find no parallel in the life of a first-century man from Nazareth. Also, the concept of imitation is itself enclosed within a larger account of participation, for which we need to be attentive to pneumatology and not just Christology.

Conclusion

This chapter has given a brief overview of some of the developments that have taken place in Pauline scholarship in recent decades. It has been far from exhaustive, and readers may wish that other debates had been discussed or other scholars mentioned. Those dealt with here are the ones that I consider to be most important in providing context for the present study, not least because these approaches have become quite influential at the level of popular theology.

All of the approaches discussed in this chapter have brought something helpful and important to the study of Paul and his understanding of the gospel. The New Perspective of Wright and others rightly challenges an overly simplistic way of thinking about Jewish legalism and how this is to be related to Paul's teaching on righteousness. The virtue-based approaches have helped to shift discussions about Christian ethics toward the holistic transformation of the agent into a morally good person. The "thoroughgoing grace" account of Campbell and others acknowledges the decisive centrality of the Christ event as an act of divine initiative and deliverance. The study of imitation has highlighted the extent to which the NT authors direct their readers to consider the life and teaching of Christ and not just to think of his death and resurrection as the basis for their forgiveness.

For the most part, my criticisms of these approaches have simply anticipated what I will go on to say in the chapters that follow as we turn to the study of Paul. What we can single out as a factor common in all of them, however, is that they do not deal adequately with the radically different concept of moral identity or agency that is at work in Paul's writings. They may work with a standard view of the self as a moral agent (as does most virtue theory) or with a largely functional account of Paul's "in Christ" language as designating the dynamic relationships within Christian community (as do the New Perspective and the imitation approaches), or they may absorb the Christian into Christ's decisive action in a way that negates any importance to the Christian's own acts of faith or goodness (as does the perfected-grace approach). Other NT scholars are sharply sensitive to the need to speak of Christian agency in carefully redescribed terms,[49] so this is not a sweeping comment about all contemporary scholarship. It is particularly a feature of these approaches. At key points in the remaining chapters, I will draw attention to the differences between Paul's way of representing the Christian life (at least, as I understand it) and these scholarly approaches. I leave it to the reader to be alert to the ways in which such approaches to Paul have made their way into the popular discourse of the church.

49. See Barclay, *Paul and the Gift*, 150; Eastman, *Paul and the Person*.

2

Who Am I Really?

Paul's Moral Crisis

Let me begin with the assertion that I am going to defend in the
rest of this book through a close reading of Paul's Epistles. This
assertion is not a new one and has been an important part of
Christian thought through the centuries, but its proper centrality to
our thinking about Christian moral life has been compromised by
decades of thinning or declining theology, especially at the popular
level within evangelicalism. The assertion is this:

> Paul represents the Great Exchange that lies at the heart of the gospel,
> whereby Jesus bears the affliction of our condition and we enjoy the
> glory of his, as involving at its most basic level an exchange not merely
> of *status* but of *identity*. It is not *simply* that our guilt is transferred
> to Jesus and his righteousness to us but that our status before God
> rests on a more fundamental exchange. What Jesus takes to the cross
> is *who we are*, our very selves with all their guilt, and what we enjoy in
> union with him is precisely *who he is*, his fullness with all its glory. The
> activity of the Spirit in sanctification, then, is intended not to bring
> about a better version of ourselves but to realize in us the personal
> moral identity of Jesus Christ. Any account of the Christian moral
> life, any program of discipleship, that does not begin and resolve with

Paul's words, "I no longer live, but Christ lives in me," is deficient and will eventually turn into a form of idolatry.

That may be a rather dense opening statement, and if you are struggling to follow it, bear with me through the course of this chapter. It will begin to make better sense as we look at some of the details of Paul's writing. It is important, though, to highlight up front how this contrasts with popular accounts of the gospel, including those that characterize much contemporary evangelicalism.[1] These fall very far short of both Paul and the Reformed articulations of the gospel that Paul proclaimed, which center on the concept of union with Christ.

Evangelicalism popularly works with an account that runs along the following lines: The death of Jesus pays for our sins, takes the punishment that we deserve, and makes it possible for us to be right with God; once we are right with God, we receive the Holy Spirit, who (or perhaps "which") functions as a kind of Gatorade, an energy shot that gives an ability to live in obedience to God's commandments that we did not have previously, to raise our moral game, as it were. We still continue to need the cross, because even in this new life of obedience, we continue to fall into sins that need to be paid for, but the transformation of our lives—sanctification—is something that comes through our moral partnership with the Spirit.

We might not render it in quite such crude terms, but this is what our account of the gospel often boils down to. The problem with it is not so much that it is wrong, but that it isn't right enough (which is generally the issue with problematic theologies: they often affirm the right things, but not enough of the right things, so that what they affirm rightly is bent out of shape by its lack of context or its skewed emphases). The problem with this, which we will consider throughout this book, is twofold.

First, it has a wrong view of the Christian self: it assumes that "I" am the principal agent of obedience, even if I need to be helped or energized by the Spirit, and doesn't take seriously enough that

1. The way I am using the word "evangelical(ism)" here is intended simply to label the subculture and its popular forms, highlighting that it does not necessarily sustain the theological heritage that lies behind it.

there is no "I" left to speak of in the Christian life, at least not in self-subsistent terms. If we begin with Paul's identification—"I no longer live, but Christ lives in me" (Gal. 2:20, my trans.)—then a very different way of speaking about the Christian moral life must emerge, one recognizing that I am being changed not into a better version of myself but into a participant in the radically "other" goodness of Jesus Christ. This helps us to see the second problem: this account works with a deficient understanding of the Spirit, seen as a kind of independent force of transformation rather than as the one who very specifically realizes the moral presence of Jesus in our lives.

This twofold problem involves a functional neglect of the place of Jesus, not just in the realization of *forgiveness* but also in the realization of *sanctification*. Properly, the gospel of Jesus Christ is not just the entry point into the kingdom of God or the locus for recovery from daily sins but is the very constitution of the kingdom itself. To put it differently, it is not just *how* we get saved; it is *what* we are saved into and what we become within that reality. We are saved "in Christ," and in Christ we do "good works" (Eph. 2:10); these are done not by independent centers of identity, by people who can say "with the help of the Spirit *I* can obey," but by those who collectively say "I no longer live, but Christ lives in me."

One of the crucial themes that will emerge in our discussion is this: any other account of Christian obedience will, in some sense, commodify righteousness. It will make goodness something I do, on the basis of which I acquire some kind of capital with God or in the eyes of God's people. That, we will see, is what legalism does, and its problem is not simply that it is naive concerning the scale of the sin that corrupts our lives and compromises our ability to obey—which is how legalism is often considered—but it does not understand the most basic category of Christian identity: who we are and why this *must* be determined by the phrase "in Christ." And this is why, at a certain point, Paul considers legalism to constitute a different gospel, something that is fundamentally sub-Christian: it involves a way of thinking about moral activity that is functionally separate from the presence of Jesus.

This book will explore the theme of Christian moral identity, with particular reference to Paul. I focus on Paul because so much of our theology is rightly drawn from the categories and imagery of his writings. Certainly, it is always vital that we set any given text or corpus of writings within the wider context of the NT so that our theologies are not skewed unwittingly by our commitment to a "canon within the canon." But it is also vital that we seek to be attentive to the movements of thought in each biblical writer on his own terms. Paul's Epistles have played a key role in the development of Christian theologies of discipleship over the centuries, and rightly so: they contain explicit and direct teaching on what it means to think and act rightly in the light of what has been revealed in Jesus Christ. However, they have also been badly misread, particularly at a popular level. I do not share the opinion that the great figures of the Reformation misread Paul, which is a claim that has been prominent in much NT scholarship in recent decades.[2] I do think, though, that the churches occupying part of the legacy of the Reformation today—the various families of evangelical churches—have widely failed to maintain what the Reformers saw so clearly: that every part of our hope is constituted by the same thing, by Jesus Christ.

In this chapter, I will trace some of the core movements in Paul's theology of Christian identity, principally seeking to remind us of how shocking some of his language is, since it has been rather muted by familiarity. It has become the kind of language that we use without thinking of its real significance. I recall a conversation with the theologian Julie Canlis, who comes from an evangelical tradition similar to my own. She pointed out we could remove the expression "in Christ" from many of the sentences in which we use it, in conversation or in prayer, *because it is not essential to their meaning*; nothing would be lost from those sentences if we were to remove the expression, because it does not bear any real load in our thoughts. It is an empty idiom, one that we use casually and thoughtlessly, much like we use expressions such as "at the end of the day" or "to be honest." Our use of these expressions does not deliberately position a thought against alternatives (i.e., something less final than "the

2. This claim lies at the heart of the New Perspective on Paul, as represented in the work of E. P. Sanders, N. T. Wright, and James D. G. Dunn. For details of their work and for some of the critiques of their representation of Luther, see under "The New Perspective on Paul" in chap. 1.

end of the day" or something less than "honest"); we use them as low-level turns of speech that could be discarded from the sentence without altering its meaning. But union with Christ is not reducible to a turn of speech, even if it should be the idiom of the Christian life. This chapter will, I hope, show this to be the case and bring to the surface the determinative significance that the expression "in Christ" has within Paul's thought.

I need to make two cautionary points before I continue. First, I am not trying to give a comprehensive theology of Christian identity or of sanctification. Both of these are larger topics, and what I am talking about here is just one thread of them. I do consider this thread to be the vital one, without which everything else unravels, and will offer some further reflections on this in the final chapter of this book. Even there, though, I will not seek to give a systematic account of either identity or sanctification. Second, as a NT scholar, I see my task as drawing attention to the details of the NT texts and considering these details afresh. However, this information must be set within a framework of classical trinitarian theology. Because of the constraints of this book, I will not have space to do this at every point, but I do want to state from the beginning that the neglect of such theology, both in academic biblical studies and in popular evangelicalism, has had a devastating effect on concepts of discipleship. At specific points in this book, I will draw attention to particular examples.

Philippians 3: Decommodified Righteousness

It may be useful to begin our reflections by listening to what Paul says about how he formerly viewed his own identity and his relationship to righteousness and the shift that occurred because of his encounter with Jesus.

> For we are the circumcision, who worship by the Spirit of God and glory in Christ Jesus and put no confidence in the flesh—though I myself have reason for confidence in the flesh also. If anyone else thinks he has reason for confidence in the flesh, I have more: circumcised on the eighth day, of the people of Israel, of the tribe of Benjamin, a Hebrew of Hebrews; as to the law, a Pharisee; as to zeal, a persecutor of the

church; as to righteousness under the law, blameless. But whatever
gain I had, I counted as loss for the sake of Christ. Indeed, I count
everything as loss because of the surpassing worth of knowing Christ
Jesus my Lord. For his sake I have suffered the loss of all things and
count them as rubbish, in order that I may gain Christ and be found
in him, not having a righteousness of my own that comes from the
law, but that which comes through faith in Christ, the righteousness
from God that depends on faith. (Phil. 3:3–9)

A few things are noteworthy here. First, although it is not necessarily conspicuous in any translation, the passage is largely devoid
of finite verbs. We generally encounter verbless or participial clauses,
almost functioning like badges: "a Hebrew of Hebrews," "of the
tribe of Benjamin," "a persecutor of the church." This is the case
until we reach verse 7, where we encounter two temporally specific
verbs. What "was gain"[3] to Paul he has "come to consider"[4] a loss (my
trans.). Something has changed. While at least some of the badges
may remain true of Paul and may continue to be valid descriptions of
his flesh (he cannot cease to be ethnically of the tribe of Benjamin),
his evaluation of them has changed at the most basic level, and what
led to this change was Jesus himself: Paul specifies that it is "because
of Christ" (*dia ton Christon*) that he has come to think differently.

Second, the passage is dense with the language of possession or
ownership, and it deploys this language in ways that change in correspondence to the change of attitude just noted. At the beginning
of the passage, for example, Paul indicates that he is someone who
"has" reasons to be confident in the flesh (3:4). The word he uses is
a participle of the verb *echō* (to have). We might reasonably, if awk-
wardly, translate this as "haver" or "possessor of": "I am a possessor
of more." Paul is an "owner" of reasons to be confident in the flesh,
and his capital exceeds that of others: "I [*egō*] have more."

But verse 7 involves a flip of attitudes toward these things. Whatever Paul previously considered to have capital value, albeit symbolic

3. The verb is *ēn*, a simple past tense from the verb "to be."
4. The verb here, *hēgēmai*, is in the perfect tense, indicating that something has
happened to bring about a new set of evaluative circumstances for Paul. He now
thinks differently about the things in question.

capital value, he now considers a capital deficit: what had been to him gain is now loss. Strikingly, in verse 8, Paul asserts this further by reusing the root *echō* in the compound participle *hyperechōn* (from *hyperechō*)—the "surpassing worth" that he associates with Jesus. If we rather stiffly translate this word as "hyper-having," we can see more of the contrast that he now makes: Paul used to consider himself to "have more" than others, but now he sees all of that perceived capital in relation to the "hyper-having" of Jesus.

The construction is interesting: this hyper-having is directed toward "the knowledge of Christ Jesus my Lord [*tēs gnōseōs Christou Iēsou tou kyriou mou*], because of whom [*di' hon*]" Paul has lost all things (3:8, my trans.). We have here a parallel construction to the one we saw in the previous verse. There it is because of Christ that Paul now considers his gains to be losses, but now a key place is occupied very specifically by the concept of the "knowledge of Christ." This genitive is ambiguous: it could be objective (knowledge concerning Jesus, or Paul's knowing of him) or subjective (Jesus's own knowledge, or his knowledge of Paul). Certainly in 1 Cor. 13:12 Paul speaks of the priority of divine knowledge in the relationship of Christians to their Lord: "For now we see in a mirror dimly, but then face to face. Now I know in part; then I shall know fully, even as I have been fully known." Here the context points in the direction of the objective reading: what Paul prioritizes is his own knowledge of Jesus. This is clearly articulated at the end of verse 8, where having reevaluated his gains as "rubbish"—actually, as the kind of rubbish that pollutes you, makes you unclean[5]—Paul now expresses his goal in terms of gaining Christ.

I want to highlight the play of language in verse 8 around the idea of ownership. The core verb is the aorist subjunctive *kerdēsō* (set in a purposive construction that is flagged by the conjunctive *hina*); this is the verbal cognate to the noun that Paul has already used for "gain" (*kerdē*). The play is important: where previously Paul had been concerned to amass achievements that could be associated with himself, with his physically particular self, his flesh—symbolic things,

---

5. Paul labels them as *skybala*, a word that suggests the uncleanness of garbage or even feces.

undoubtedly, that would function as moral or social capital—now he considers his hope to lie in acquiring a person, Jesus. He elaborates on this with another interesting play of language: when he acquires Christ, it is not that Jesus will be his newest and best possession, the latest trophy in his collection, but that he will be found in Christ, his self-subsistence surrendered to Jesus. I trust that this is clear: the normal expectation of the verb *kerdainō* is that it will point to the acquisition of something that is now owned by the subject, but here the subject gains something that actually takes ownership of him. Paul's shift can be stated like this: I used to wish that people and God would look at me, with all my physical particularity, and see how much I had that would speak of my status within God's kingdom; now I want them to look at me and see that my particular self is in Christ's self, that what I have is, in truth, what he has.

This leads in to one of the famous *pistis Christou* verses, 3:9, where scholars have debated whether they are dealing with a subjective genitive, in which Paul speaks of the faith (or fidelity) exercised by Jesus, or an objective genitive, in which Jesus is the object of our faith.[6] Despite some prominent advocates of the subjective interpretation (which does have some validity within the context), the balance of NT scholarship still favors the classic objective view, that this is about faith *in* Jesus. That the parallel genitive construction of *gnōseōs Christou* (3:8) appears to be objective supports the same interpretation here (3:9): it makes sense contextually that Jesus is represented as the object of Paul's attention, and this need not be considered to wrongly prioritize a human act, because it is affirmed as part of a language play in which Paul subordinates his activity of reaching for Jesus to Christ's ultimate acquisition of him.

The key is the contrast that Paul establishes in verse 9 between his old way of thinking—that he could have a righteousness of his own that is "from the law"[7]—and his new way of thinking, where his

6. For an overview of this debate, see Bird and Sprinkle, *Faith of Jesus Christ*. See also the discussion under "The Apocalyptic Paul, the Perfection of Grace, and the Faith of Jesus Christ" in chap. 1.

7. The expression he uses in 3:9 is *mē echōn emēn dikaiosynēn tēn ek nomou* (not having a righteousness that is mine from the law). The use of the possessive is vital to the flow of thought. What he disavows is any sense of ownership of this righteousness.

righteousness is not his own but someone else's. It has come to him through his relationship to that other person; it is *dia pisteōs Christou*. Now Paul's righteousness—his moral capital—is not of himself but of God[8] and comes to him by the mediation of Jesus. The place of faith is affirmed in this, for the word occurs twice in close succession and in different cases: God's righteousness comes "through the faith of Christ" and is "upon faith" (*epi tē pistei*). However we might relate these expressions to the fidelity of Jesus—and I want to reiterate that our continuing affirmation of the doctrine of justification by faith should not obscure the importance of Jesus's fidelity in God's work of salvation—the language resonates with the emphasis found more widely in Paul's writings that we are, characteristically, "believers."

From this expressed purpose, most modern translations represent verse 10 as if it starts a new sentence that effectively restates this: "I want to know Christ—yes, to know the power of his resurrection" (3:10 NIV). Actually, though, the verse starts with an articular infinitive that is in the genitive case; that is, it appears to be part of the same chain of genitives that links righteousness to God through Christ: righteousness is "of God" and "of the knowledge of Christ." These are not two discrete sources of righteousness or even complementary parts of it. Rather, they co-inhere: to know Christ is to have the righteousness of God.

Paul's inversion of his old way of thinking about righteousness as a commodity he can possess continues in verse 12, after he has spoken about being conformed to Christ in his death and resurrection. The language he uses here is highly suggestive of these inversions: "Not that I have already laid hold [of it], or have already been made perfect, but I pursue [*diōkō*] and overtake/lay hold of [it], because Christ Jesus has laid hold of me" (my trans.). Here is the inversion: Paul now recognizes that he can "lay hold of" this righteousness only because the Righteous One, Christ, has "laid hold" of him. The same verb, *katalambanō*, is used of both. Only because he is owned by Christ can he now possess righteousness. The problem before was not that righteousness was beyond his grasp but that he was simply not constitutionally eligible to possess it. To experience it, he had to

---

8. It is *tēn ek theou dikaiosynēn*.

be incorporated into Christ. Interestingly, the word that Paul uses for his new pursuit of this righteousness is the same word that he previously used of his persecution of the church: *diōkō*. Paul is not inert in his union with Christ. His righteousness is passive in the sense that he is the objective recipient of another person's goodness, but that passivity is not the same as inertia: he pursues righteousness with a renewed zeal now that he knows it is something he can enjoy only through his fellowship with another.

At the risk of belaboring something that may already be sufficiently evident, let me note that Paul has shifted both from seeing righteousness as a kind of moral or social capital that he can acquire and possess and from seeing himself as an entity autonomously capable of acquiring such capital. He now sees righteousness as something that he can possess only if he allows himself to be "re-identified" with someone else, with Jesus. He now sees that it can be amassed not by doing things or being a particular kind of person but only by knowing someone and by being known by that one.

Now, this articulation of Paul's old "legalistic" way of thinking about righteousness in relation to his new one is not quite the same as our standard ways of thinking about the problem of legalism. We have typically described the problem of legalism or of "works righteousness" in terms of a balance sheet: the legalist thinks in terms of a performed obedience to the commandments that will keep them in credit with God, not recognizing how profound their inability to enact such obedience really is. There is, I think, a real question about whether any Jew of the Second Temple period was ever a card-carrying legalist in quite these terms. Aside from anything else, it works with an economic model of a bank account that was entirely alien to most people of the time, for whom money was a limited part of their wealth (if they had any) and their economic interactions. The mental image that we use today is really a modern, post–Adam Smith way of thinking about individual wealth and credit within an economy. The language of capital or commodity that I am using allows for something that is just as real but less limited to a particular set of modern economic practices. It recognizes that there is such a thing as symbolic or social capital, which is associated with the perception of our status not just with God but also with the various communities in which we live and operate. It is not as straightforward as a credit sheet, since some of the elements cannot be easily quantified, but within a given community, it will say whether you are an insider or an outsider and where you might rank within the group. It will affect how others treat you and how you benefit from these interactions. Someone who has high levels of social capital will enjoy the favor (and perhaps the favors)[9] of others, as these people look to benefit from that capital by association. It is this perception of social capital that governs the dynamics of high school groups and cliques; it is the same perception that makes some people influential. In some cultures and economies it is explicit; in others it is tacit. There is, moreover, a blurring of the audiences who are held to evaluate our performative capital: we might hold it to be something we have done to please and honor God and might be absolutely convinced in ourselves that it has been rendered to him as service, but in reality the audience that scores us may be a human one. The gallery to which we play may be filled with other people.

The Pharisaical preoccupation with "badging" (or "boundary-maintaining") practices like ritual washing, circumcision, or table purity is easily explicable within such an approach: in the context of a highly variegated Judaism, these very public practices allow us to identify the insider, the real Jew, from the outsider, the Jew whose conduct is questionable with respect to the law. Paul's zeal to persecute the church, meanwhile, might be particularly noteworthy, marking him out as someone who deserves a level of deference within the Pharisaical community.

9. This notion of honor and its association with symbolic capital has been a prominent element in the social-scientific study of the NT, which draws heavily on the discipline of social anthropology. See Malina, *New Testament World*, chap. 1. Recently John Barclay (*Paul and the Gift*) has drawn on the anthropological study of gift-giving in his examination of Paul's distinctive account of the divine gift of salvation. Contrary to our modern assumptions about what gifts are and represent, Barclay and the historians/anthropologists on whom he draws highlight that gifts were (and are!) given as part of an economy of favor to people who could be expected to return a favor in some way at a later stage. This can be as significant to social functioning as a monetary economy and actually more significant on a day-to-day basis in economies outside the modern, developed world. Crucially, such economies of gift-giving involve constant, but often tacit, decisions about the worth or value of the person to whom a gift is given. Their social capital or symbolic capital is always being evaluated.

But for these dynamics to work, there must be some perception that the self in question can acquire status or capital against its own name. If that assumption is disrupted and the person recognizes that they are now identified by the name of someone else—the name of the person into whom they have been baptized—then the whole endeavor is altered. If we take seriously that all we accomplish truly belongs to the name of another and that all we enjoy is a function of *his* wealth and not ours, then the dynamics of our social identity will change accordingly.

Galatians 2:20 and Context: Incorporated Identity

From our discussion of Phil. 3, we can now turn to Gal. 2:20 and its wider context. The letter is, of course, preoccupied with a movement in the Galatian church that is pressing for a particular form of adherence to the law and its customs. While there may be debates about what precisely this entailed, there is no doubt about the basic problem. Paul's condemnation of the movement excludes any sense that we are dealing with mere differences of opinion on this or that issue: this is "a different gospel" (Gal. 1:6). Paul is quick to qualify this comment by saying that there is really only one thing that can *truly* be labeled as the *euangelion*, but he then continues by warning about the preaching of an account of salvation that is different from this: "But even if we or an angel from heaven should preach to you a gospel contrary to the one we preached to you, let him be accursed" (Gal. 1:8). Paul calls this a different gospel because it is premised upon something different, and I want to highlight how Paul represents this basic difference of premise as a matter of identity: it is not just about what we do or how we do it but about who we are and how we conceive of ourselves.

The key verse here will be Gal. 2:20, but there are few things that are helpful to note in the buildup to it. First, as Paul introduces the autobiographical account that will dominate the first two chapters of the letter, he makes explicit that he is seeking to please not people but God and that his message does not originate within human contexts but has been disclosed to him in the revelation of Jesus Christ.

This acknowledges the human and social dimension of the problem that we discussed when looking at Philippians: Paul sets his message over against that of his opponents precisely on the basis of its origin outside the circles of pious community. This invites us to think about the problem that he addresses not as something that is exclusively or even principally oriented toward God, which are the terms in which we often describe legalism, but as something governed more by social conventions, by how those around us think about us and think about what it means to be an insider or an outsider of the holy community. Second, what Paul sets against the false gospel is precisely an autobiography, a narrative of his experience and its contribution to his identity. Galatians 1:13–14 recounts something of what he saw to be his social capital within his earlier life in the Jewish community, a brief description that we can fill out from our discussion of Philippians. In fact, it is interesting that his description of his advancement is specified to be "in Judaism" (*en tō Ioudaismō*). This is one of the few points in ancient literature where this word appears, and its use here points to the social or human dimension of his advancement. It is rather like someone saying, "I advanced in Christianity," or (perhaps better) "in evangelicalism": it points to the culture and society of the religion rather than to its content. But this narrative of progress and social advancement that Paul told himself in his former life is disrupted by the revelation of the Son: Paul sees not some*thing* but some*one* who changes him, and nothing can be the same afterward.

Given what we have just noted, Paul describes himself as effectively shunning the advice of other people of flesh and blood; he absents himself from the input of a religious community. What follows is a narrative that continues to affirm the danger of seeking to please people: even Peter (Cephas, Gal. 2:11) is challenged for his hypocrisy (2:13) of "not walking with the truth of the gospel" (2:14, my trans.) as he acts out of fear of the circumcision party (2:12). It is noteworthy that here Paul is concerned with a "functional" legalism: these are actions and practices that contradict the gospel, not necessarily theological articulations of the view that we will be saved by works. This takes us back to a point that I have now made several times: legalism is not necessarily a card-carrying, principled commitment to the idea that one will be saved by one's works. Rather, it is a way of thinking and acting that pursues religious capital.

One of the easily overlooked features of this autobiography is the frequency with which the first-person singular is used: the narrative is full of references to "I" and "me" (even if these are found in the endings of verbs, rather than in pronouns—there are, in fact, very few of these). This is not self-importance on Paul's part, I think, and neither is it just a feature of the autobiographical character of the text. Instead, I think it is building deliberately toward what Paul says in 2:20: "I no longer live, but Christ lives in me" (my trans.). Having used the first person throughout the narrative, he now in effect says, "But there is no 'me' to speak of, at least not in simple terms." Read in this way, verse 20 is something of a punch line to the autobiography that has been recounted through the letter.

Before we get to that punch line, however, Paul adds a key piece of discussion, which may (or may not) reproduce part of his conversation with Peter. He asserts what appears to be a belief held in common by both:

> We ourselves are Jews by birth and not Gentile sinners; yet we know that a person is not justified by works of the law but through faith in Jesus Christ, so we also have believed in Christ Jesus, in order to be justified by faith in Christ and not by works of the law, because by works of the law no one will be justified. (Gal. 2:15–16)

The next verse (17) makes clear that there will continue to be sin, even in those who are justified in Christ, and that this in no way makes Christ a servant of sin. The persistence of sin, though, appears to be a factor prompting the emergence of a group who advocates a certain mode of obedience to the law. At least, it is the context for Paul's next statement, which really takes us into the heart of things: "For if I rebuild what I tore down, I prove myself to be a transgressor. For through the law I died to the law, so that I might live to God" (Gal. 2:18–19). Now we are getting near to the point: a death has taken place through the processes built into the law that has resulted in a new relationship to the law. Remarkably, this death is Paul's own: "I died." This is what is then unpacked in our key verse: "I have been crucified with Christ. It is no longer I who live, but Christ who lives in me. And the life I now live in the flesh I live by faith in the Son of God, who loved me and gave himself for me" (Gal. 2:20). So Paul has died, but this death has happened through his union with Jesus and the corresponding participation in Christ's own death. Within his understanding of the gospel, the death of Christ is not just representative as he bears the sinner's guilt and takes the sinner's place, but it is incorporative, and what is incorporated is Paul himself. Insofar as he participates also in the resurrection, it is because the same Christ with whom he died now lives in him as a new reality that inhabits his flesh. His own flesh, then, no longer defines the limits of his existence or constitutes the true outline of his self; he is in Christ and Christ is in him.

In the Scottish Highlands where I grew up, there is a colloquial expression that is often used in response to the question "How are you?" The common reply to this is "You're seeing it." This expression indicates that what you see before you, this flesh, is me, and you can see with your eyes how I am. Paul's point is that what you see with your eyes when looking at his physical self is not "it"; there is more, and the possibilities and goals of his life are now defined by *that* reality and not by the limits of the lump of matter that he once considered to be the entirety of Paul and to be worth all of his investments. It is not that there is no such person as "Paul" anymore; he still uses the first-person singular throughout this autobiographical account, he still draws upon all the abilities that he acquired through his life within Judaism, and he still writes to the Galatians as "Paul, an apostle." But Paul is now Paul-in-Christ; Paul-in-himself is a thing of the past. We might even translate Gal. 2:20 as "I live, yet not I, but Christ lives in me."[10]

Immediately afterward Paul starts to speak about the Spirit and in a way that singles out the Spirit as a particular marker of salvation: "This alone I wish to ask you: Did you receive the Spirit from the works of the law or from the hearing of faith?" (Gal. 3:2, my trans.). This is a dense and important verse. Paul focuses on the reality of the Spirit (and again, note that he is speaking to people who have

10. The underlying Greek of 2:20 is *zō de ouketi egō, zē de en emoi Christos.*

received the Spirit, not to those outside the community of salvation)
and asks whether the Spirit has come from the "works of the law" or
from the "hearing of faith." I translate that last expression clumsily
but literally because I want to bring out its force: it is sometimes
translated as "believing what you heard" or as "hearing with faith,"
but I think these renderings mask the nature of the contrast. The
word that I have translated as "hearing" is *akoē*; we get our word
"acoustics" from this root. It is a noun designating something that
has been heard; we would normally use it not for a message that
has been written and read but for one that we have listened to. We
might even translate it "the acoustics of faith," since it is linked to
the genitive of the noun *pistis*.

The crucial element is that there exist two different ways of relating
to the thing mentioned in the two contrastive parts of this question:
Do you get the Spirit as a performer of the works of the law or as
a listener to the acoustics of faith? Here is the subtle point: the first
makes you the principal agent (the performer of the works of the
law), and the other makes you into someone who appropriates the
performance of someone else (the one who listens to the acoustics of
faith). One makes you the owner of what is achieved, the proprietor
of righteous acts; the other makes you a beneficiary of the virtuosity
of another person.

Paul, then, is effectively asking: Did you earn the Spirit, or did
you receive the Spirit by listening to what someone else has done
or is doing? This leads to a further contrast: "If you started with
the Spirit [whom you received by the hearing of faith], are you now
finishing with the flesh?" (3:3, my trans.). You "got in" by believing
and receiving the Spirit; "are you so foolish" (3:3a) that you think you
are supposed to "stay in" and to finish in a different way,[11] by going
back to the old way of thinking that *you* are the principal agent, that
it is about your performance, done by your flesh?

11. My language here deliberately echoes the famous terminology of Sanders and
the New Perspective and does so in order to highlight the ironic similarities between
this way of describing Jewish attitudes toward grace and those of much contemporary
Christianity, where we are happy to speak of getting into the kingdom through Christ,
but staying in the kingdom is then something we do by rigorous obedience. See the
discussion in chap. 1, "Scholarly Contexts for the Present Study."

Pause for a moment and reflect on Paul's audience and his claims about them. He is not writing to unconverted Jews or to someone who might say, "From start to finish we are saved by obeying the law." He is writing to people who have entered salvation by believing and have received the Spirit, and he is saying to them, "Your theology about how one 'gets in' is fine, but your theology about how one then proceeds stinks, precisely because it does not recognize that the gospel defines life in the kingdom in the same way that it defines entry into it. You 'get in' and you 'stay in' by participating in the same reality: Jesus Christ, known through the hearing of faith, present by the work of the Spirit." All of the above Paul directs to "born again" Christians, evangelicals who have initially received the gospel by faith. It has the capacity, therefore, to cut to the core of evangelicalism today.

Paul goes on to recount where the law is properly located within the sweep of God's work of redemption and where the death of Jesus is located with respect to the law. For the sake of space, I will pass over this material, simply noting its emphasis that the law had (and has) a particular function to discipline and condemn and that prior to the coming of Christ, God's people lived under it while also enslaved to the elemental principles of the world. We will consider this language in more depth in chapter 3. Here I simply want to note that Paul represents the gospel as involving two inseparable sendings. When the fullness of time came (4:4), God sent his Son, born into the same conditions as others—born of a woman, born under the law—to redeem them from those conditions (4:5): the minors become heirs, adopted as children of God. This sending is causally connected (by the conjunction *hoti*) to the paired sending of the Spirit into our hearts (4:6): it is "because you are sons" that God sent the Spirit.[12] Note also, though, something that we might skim over too quickly: the Spirit is specified to be "the Spirit of his Son" (*to pneuma tou hiou autou*), and he generates a correspondence between our selves and the self of the Son—by him we cry "Abba, Father." We are not here imitating Jesus but participating in him and in his unique relationship

---

12. The gendered term "sons" has to be retained in translation, rather than using the gender-neutral "children" (though Paul does shift to using the latter word at points in Rom. 8, as we will see in chap. 6) because our filial relationship to God is a participation in the relationship of the Son to his Father.

to the Father. We are, to use the language that Paul employs in 3:26–27
(alt.), "sons of God through faith" who have "put on Christ" in our
baptism. This statement leads into a description of the community of
faith that is often robbed of its real significance: "There is no longer
a Jew or a Greek, there is no longer a slave or a free person, there is
no longer a male and a female; for all of you are one in Christ Jesus"
(Gal. 3:28, my trans.). I have added indefinite articles to the normal
translation of the verse. This is a valid translation of the Greek,
and it helps to bring out the sense that these particularities are all
still present but that they are enclosed within a larger reality that
constitutes a more basic identity, shared by all participants: you are
all one in Christ. One can imagine Paul saying this in a room filled
with a mixture of people (some of whom may be tacitly evaluating
and judging others) and pointing at each person: a Jew, a Greek, a
slave, a free person. The differences are not obliterated, but they are
no longer considered to be the most basic elements of identity.

What I am seeking to highlight is this: the shift that takes place
in the gospel is represented by Paul in terms of identity, of who we
are. We are redefined, re-identified, by our incorporation into Christ.
This is the basis for his righteousness being imputed to us; it is not
a transaction that occurs between external parties, Jesus and the
Father, but an incorporation into a person whose relationship with
God is perfect. And the Spirit who inhabits us is not an energizing
infusion of power; he is very specifically Christ's Spirit, who makes
his goodness a reality in our limbs. Entry into the kingdom and moral
identity *within* the kingdom are both defined and constituted by the
identity of Jesus. The same gospel rules both.

We cannot, then, think about the Christian moral life as something
"I" do, assisted in some sense by the Spirit. It is something that Christ-
in-me does; he is as much the acting subject of my verbs of obedience
as I am. As soon as we lose sight of this, we move toward a way of
thinking about righteousness that commodifies obedience, makes it
into something I achieve and accrue, rather than something I inhabit
as I inhabit Jesus. And yet, this is exactly what happens widely in
evangelical thought today, exacerbated in some circles by a tendency
to isolate the kingship (or kingdom) of Jesus from its wider context
of union with Christ. Jesus is represented as the one to whom we

are to render our obedience, whose reign we are to proclaim to the world and to reflect in our own lives. That is good, but it is only one side of the account, for we cannot render obedience to Jesus the king unless we clothe ourselves with Jesus the servant.

Conclusion

This chapter has laid some foundations for the rest of the book by drawing attention to the way Paul represents Christian moral identity as "in Christ." We have sketched some elements that we will fill out in later chapters and have made some points whose significance remains to be explored. Let me draw a few initial conclusions.

First, it should be obvious that any efforts to "sort" or "fix" moral problems within the church that are based on *our* performance of certain activities have overlooked the basic question of identity that needs to contextualize who "we" are in Christ. By this I am saying not that there is no room for Christian moral effort or the formation of good Christian habits but that these need to be done with proper awareness that "I no longer live, but Christ lives in me." For example, the routine of having a daily quiet time is a good thing, but not if it is considered a thing in itself.

Second, and following from this, fostering Christian moral identity is not principally about instilling good habits or establishing norms that mark our community but about fostering a person's sense of who Christ is in them and who they are in Christ. This, I think, is one of the reasons why the sacraments of baptism and the Lord's Supper are so important within the NT and are frequently appealed to by Paul for moral purposes. Our next two chapters will consider this in more depth, but here we can simply say that the task of forming Christian moral identity is not about saying "Do not handle, Do not taste, Do not touch" (Col. 2:21) but about helping believers to know the significance of being baptized into the death of Jesus and united to him in his resurrection. Christian moral identity is formed when we routinely enact a celebratory memory of an appalling death.

Third, these elements are not additional to salvation or justification but belong to the same act of identification by which justification is accomplished. The account of righteousness that Paul comes to hold as a follower of Christ involves a classically conceived notion of justification by faith. But it is vital to recognize that at stake is not just a level of righteousness we cannot reach by ourselves but our whole mode of relationship to what we label "righteousness." Righteousness is no longer to be conceived as something that any believer will own as a form of capital that they have acquired through lineage or labor; rather, it is now seen as something they enjoy through their identification with someone else.

Our theological language of "imputation" is actually a way of speaking about a mode of acquisition that originates outside ourselves. The point for us is that Paul links this acquisition to the concept of selfhood: because we are "in Christ," his righteousness becomes ours. Imputation is, if you like, a corollary of implantation. What this means for the righteousness that is manifest in the transformation of our Christian lives is that it proceeds not from an infusion of new spiritual energy but from our new identities constituted in union with Jesus Christ. It may, perhaps, be helpful to consider some of the clichés that we often use of the Christian life. We rightly warn against the danger of seeking to do something "in our own strength," directing people to "rely on God." But if these admonitions are not carefully considered, they can sound like we just need some assistance, a shot of energy from outside that will enhance our deficit of strength. This is why I suggested that our popular ways of thinking about the Spirit often understand him as functioning as an energy supplement. That, coincidentally, was broadly how the Spirit was represented in some of the medieval theologies of virtue that subscribed to the concept of "infused grace"; ironically, much contemporary Protestant theology has a notion of the Spirit that is rather similar. The antidote is a right emphasis on the language of union with Christ: it is the presence of Christ, by his Spirit, that brings a change to our lives.

3

Baptism and Moral Identity

Clothing Ourselves in Christ

In this chapter and the next, we will consider the way that Paul uses the core symbolic practices of Christian community that we typically label "sacraments" to define and to nurture Christian moral identity. The theme that will run through both chapters is that Paul repeatedly draws on the symbolism and significance of the sacraments to render Christian identity and often moves from this symbolism to specific applications of how Christians should live and act. Rather than imposing a program of discipleship and development, Paul challenges his readers to reflect on the real significance of the sacraments in which they have participated or to which they have been witnesses. That significance concerns their participation in the identity of Jesus Christ, constituted by their union with him and by the activity of the Spirit to realize this participatory identification. In the next chapter, we will consider the Lord's Supper as an act of participatory remembrance that is repeated in the Christian's life. In this chapter, we will consider baptism as the initiatory rite of Christian identity by which we are redefined as those who have clothed themselves in Christ. This personal emphasis is vital to the significance of the sacrament.

Paul nowhere describes the actual *practice* of baptism; the closest we come to it is the comment he makes in 1 Cor. 1:14–16, where he indicates that he personally can only remember baptizing Crispus and Gaius in Corinth. He makes this comment in the context of stressing that it was not in his name that anyone had been baptized; he is grateful that any such perception would be confined to these two figures. Without going into detail on this, the comment reflects the close association between the act of baptism and "the name." We are baptized *eis to onoma*, "in [or, into] the name." The name in question is sometimes specified to be that of Jesus, but at the end of Matthew it is also specified to be "the name of the Father and of the Son and of the Holy Spirit" (Matt. 28:19). Some see such language simply as specifying that this is a "Jesus baptism" rather than a ritual washing associated with another figure whose name might be invoked at some point.[1] Others see the language as indicating a transfer of ownership to Jesus. Neither of these understandings really articulates the strong sense of identification with Jesus that baptism generates. In order to see this, we need to probe the associated imagery, particularly the use of clothing metaphors. Nevertheless, simply by invoking "the name" we are indicating that issues of identity are at stake: names are, after all, core elements in identity. In the wider discussion of 1 Cor. 1, this is important, for groups have formed within the church that identify themselves principally with other names—"big names," we might say—rather than with Christ himself. That is what concerns Paul so much: he doesn't want anyone to think it possible to be baptized into his name, to have an identity defined principally by Paul.

Paul uses the language and imagery of baptism in significant ways in four places: Gal. 3:27; Rom. 6:3–4; 1 Cor. 10:2; 12:13. He speaks in passing about baptism in other places, such as 1 Cor. 15:29 (where he refers to baptism of the dead) and, as we've just noted, 1 Cor. 1:14–16, but these are incidental references to events of which we cannot know the details. So I focus principally on the four main texts.

Galatians 3:27 and Context: Putting on Christ

We will start with Gal. 3:27, since it effectively picks up the thread from what we looked at in the last chapter. There we considered the

---

1. Hartman, "'Into the Name of Jesus.'"

flow of Paul's account of salvation to the point where he states, "I no longer live, but Christ lives in me" (Gal. 2:20, my trans.). From there, he engages in a lengthy account of the place of the law in relation to the gospel experience of God's people before the coming of Jesus: it governed them while they were in their minority. But now that faith has come, those who believe are no longer under its supervision.

> For in Christ Jesus you are all sons of God, through faith. For as many of you as were baptized into Christ have put on Christ. There is neither Jew nor Greek, there is neither slave nor free, there is no male and female, for you are all one in Christ Jesus. And if you are Christ's, then you are Abraham's offspring, heirs according to promise. (Gal. 3:26–29)

When we looked at this in the preceding chapter, we emphasized that Paul recontextualizes the particular identities that compose the community of faith within the constitutive identity of Jesus himself: the categories that once divided and stratified do so no longer because a more basic identity holds us together. We are all one in Christ Jesus. Here I want to note how, in this context, Paul makes particular use of baptismal imagery.

Baptism is represented as a passive act: Paul's addressees "were baptized." It is also a relocative act: they were baptized "in(to) Christ" (*eis Christon*). The tense is aorist, which points toward the particularity of the event of incorporation into Christ. This is most significant because it is paralleled in the aorist tense of the verb *enedysasthe* (you have put on/clothed yourselves with). These two verbs share a tense because they point to the same event: it is not that you were baptized into Christ *and also* (i.e., subsequently) put him on. Rather, the baptism and the putting on are the same thing. As an aside, the clothing imagery may connote the wearing of a robe in the ritual of baptism, further emphasizing the connection between the two. The word order in Greek is also suggestive. It is literally "For as many (of you) that in Christ were baptized, Christ you have put on." By word order and repetition, the emphasis falls on the personhood and identity of Jesus.

This imagery of "donning" Christ as our new identity is reflected elsewhere in the Pauline writings. Of particular note is Col. 3:8–11 (emphasis added):

> But now you must put them all away: anger, wrath, malice, slander, and obscene talk from your mouth. Do not lie to one another, *seeing that you have put off the old self with its practices and have put on the new self, which is being renewed in knowledge after the image of its creator.* Here there is not Greek and Jew, circumcised and uncircumcised, barbarian, Scythian, slave, free; but Christ is all, and in all.

Sanctification (and its corollary of mortification) is here represented as stripping off the old self (lit. "the old man") and putting on the new self ("the new man") in the image of its creator. This is the core moral image in the passage: sins are to be abandoned, not ultimately because they are contrary to the commandments but because they are contrary to our identity in Christ. The verb appears in the *middle* voice, which is often used with a reflexive sense and here designates something that we do to ourselves: we dress ourselves in Christ. There remains, then, an emphasis on the Christian life as one that involves activity and effort; we are not inert bystanders to the processes of sanctification and mortification. But the effort that we undertake is a *personal* one: we put on Christ and put off our old selves.

Both Col. 3 and Gal. 3 immediately link baptism into Christ with a formulaic way of speaking of unity within the variegated reality of the Christian community: "There is not Greek and Jew, circumcised and uncircumcised, barbarian, Scythian, slave, free; but Christ is all, and in all." This link is significant within the flow of the epistle. Paul has been challenging an emphasis on law intended to make particular distinctions, to define who is "in" and who is "out" on the basis of legal observance, but the significance of baptism cuts across this, for *whoever* has been baptized into Christ is "in" him. As we will see, that has something powerful to say concerning Christian unity and its foundations.

In Gal. 4:1–7, he frames this same transformation in terms of "adoption": we have put on Christ the Son and as a result share in his relational cry of "Abba, Father." Here Paul raises an interesting question. He asks why those who have come to enjoy this sonly[2] relationship with God—knowing him because he has known them—are turning back to their enslavement to false gods, to idolatry. He will describe these as "the weak and miserable principles/elemental spirits" (*ta asthenē kai ptōcha stoicheia*, 4:9, my trans.) and will then go on to describe the observance of special feasts and festivals, just as these were observed in Israel.

The same word for these elemental forces, *stoicheia*, is also used in Col. 2:8 and 2:20, again in the context of observing certain regulations. The term is encountered in Greek in a variety of contexts and with a range of meanings, but it usually points to things that are constituent elements of larger things, the building blocks from which they are made. The core meaning of the singular *stoicheion* is actually "one of a series," which is how it is used in ancient mathematics: it points to occupying a particular place in an order. Paul seems to use the word as if it can at once point to the physical elements of this world, a common enough meaning, and to the demonic forces that work around them, which is an overtone encountered in some ancient philosophical writing. Effectively, he says, your fleshly instincts are enslaved to the lowest things of existence, to your most beastly qualities, and as such they serve demonic forces.

In the Colossians text, Paul links the *stoicheia* to the practices of syncretism: it appears to be the case that the beliefs of many within the church in Colossae involved a mix of Jewish practice and local folk belief.[3] It is easy for us to label such syncretism as demonic, but we may not appreciate why Paul would use the same word for the forces at work in Galatia. What holds the apparently different problems seen in Colossae and Galatia together is that both are governed by the underlying dynamics of idolatry. The Colossians had a hodgepodge of religious ideas: they thought about God as if he could be manipulated,

2. *Sonly*, or *filial*, is obviously a gendered term, and this is understandably a sensitive issue for many. However, it is important that we retain this gendered dimension in our discussion throughout the book because it expresses our identity as God's adopted children specifically with reference to our participation in the Son. That is, the gendered particularity is a function of the personal particularity of the one *in whom* we are saved.

3. The point is made, though with some variations, by Arnold, *Colossian Syncretism*; and Foster, *Colossians*.

just as people thought they could control the pagan deities by magical incantations or ritual acts. But the Galatians were doing the very same thing with Yahweh, acting as if they could automatically acquire a blessing from their deity by performing the law. That is not just about giving the law greater preeminence in our lives than it should have; it is about giving the powers an authority in the world that we can coerce through capital we gain by ritual performance. Effectively, Paul says, "You are thinking about God and his law as if you were pagans, trying to keep their deities happy. That way of thinking about salvation is entirely at odds with the story that your baptism tells. Look to your baptism and see just how wrong this way of thinking is!" Baptism, understood within the narrative that he has recounted through the epistle, articulates the basic truth of Christian identity that repudiates a way of thinking about works as capital: "I no longer live, but Christ lives in me. I am clothed in Christ."

Romans 6:3–4 and Context: A Death and Life Not Our Own

Romans 6 develops the same point and presents a similar set of contextual issues. Paul has written at length about our status under the law (no one is righteous; all have fallen short) and our status in Christ (there is no condemnation for those who are in Christ Jesus). In Rom. 6 he faces the question of whether this means we can do what we like, whether this is a license for sin: "What shall we say then? Are we to continue in sin that grace may abound? By no means! How can we who died to sin still live in it?" (Rom. 6:1–2). It is at this point that Paul invokes baptism:

> Do you not know that all of us who have been baptized into Christ Jesus were baptized into his death? We were buried therefore with him by baptism into death, in order that, just as Christ was raised from the dead by the glory of the Father, we too might walk in newness of life. For if we have been united with him in a death like his, we shall certainly be united with him in a resurrection like his. We know that our old self was crucified with him in order that the body of sin might be brought to nothing, so that we would no longer be enslaved to sin. For one who has died has been set free from sin. (Rom. 6:3–7)

The construction is very similar to the one we have just seen in Gal. 3:27, in which the second clause explains something that is true of "as many as have been baptized into Christ" (alt.). In this case, the verb "baptize" is repeated in the second clause, ensuring that the reader sees their identification with the death of Jesus as an essential element of the union signified by their baptism.

It is particularly important to note that we are identified very specifically with *his* death. We often think about the symbolism of baptism as representing the "new creation" described in 2 Cor. 5:17. In the case of believers' baptism and full immersion, the act of rising from the water is often taken to symbolize the new person emerging into the world. This is fine, but it is vital to recognize that the death of the old self is not a self-contained event. Rather, it is a consequence of identification with the death of Jesus, and the life of the new person is identified with the life of Jesus. It is not that we have an old self that has been symbolically buried and a new self that has risen to replace it; we have an old self in itself that has been buried and a new self in Christ that shares in his life.

Paul goes on to stress this in the following verses, and the tenses of his verbs bear an important pastoral dimension (one to which we will return in the next two chapters): while we *have been* buried with Jesus in baptism, we *will be* like him in the resurrection. The difference hints at what we saw already in Phil. 3: "Not that I have already obtained this or am already perfect, but I press on to make it my own, because Christ Jesus has made me his own" (3:12). Paul's distinction between our present and future states has enormous pastoral importance, and we should not overlook this. Our own lives, and the lives of those in our congregations and families, continue to be marked by imperfection, and we need to remind one another about the tenses that shape the representation of the Christian life in the NT. We are often crushed by an unrealistic perfectionism that does more than just bring guilt; it also brings doubt, generated by the incongruity between what we do and what we claim. Here, though, is a window into the underlying theology that may generate such doubts: they may well come from a perception of moral performance that sees it as something "I" (as an autonomous new creation) do, rather than as something that Christ-in-me or I-in-Christ do, a reality still to be brought to its perfection.

Whether this is the case or not, the striking thing about these passages is that they invite us to identify with the past of Jesus, to make the narrative of his death our own, and in doing so they invite us to identify also with his future. Our future, the possibilities for what our selves might be and do, is no longer defined by the limits of our natural goodness but is now defined by his goodness. Our destinies are correspondingly determined. And precisely because *his* resurrection has already happened, that future is already inaugurated, even if not consummated.

Paul makes an interesting and important association between this "inaugurated eschatology" and the acting presence of the Holy Spirit. In several places he describes the Spirit as a "down payment" (*arrabōn*, 2 Cor. 1:22; 2 Cor. 5:5; Eph. 1:14) or as "firstfruits" (*aparchē*, Rom. 8:23). The first word is often translated "seal" but originally had a slightly different connotation than it might have today. The point of such language is that what we have now is of a kind with what we will have in future: it is a first installment of the reality to come in full later. In this sense our lives enjoy the presence of the future in the here and now. When Paul describes the resurrection body in 1 Cor. 15, he characterizes it as a body that is "spiritual"; this is not, I think, a description of a noncorporeal body but rather of a body fully transformed by the presence of the divine life within it.[4]

We can take genuine consolation from recognizing that our transformation is not complete and that our current moral state will not be our final one, but this can never excuse our failures and can never be used as a warrant to think lightly of sin. This is precisely Paul's point

4. Some will recognize here language that is reminiscent of Moltmann, *Theology of Hope*. While I acknowledge this, I stress that I am using this language of pneumatology and eschatology in a way that is aligned with classically conceived trinitarian monotheism, in which the distinction between creator and creation is clearly maintained. Moltmann breaks this distinction down, and my own view is that, in doing so, he loses a crucial biblical emphasis on the divine nature and sacrifices something vital to the account of salvation as truly something that comes to us from outside or from above. Kathryn Tanner (*Jesus, Humanity and the Trinity*, 10) offers some typically insightful comments on the family of approaches to which Moltmann belongs. Basically, all such approaches attenuate the very difference between God and humanity that is the ground of our hope—namely, that God is not a thing among other things but is distinctively and essentially "other."

in Rom. 6, which of course follows his discussion of justification in Rom. 5. It is simply unthinkable for us to believe that our justification by grace allows us to continue our sinful practices, for we live under the dominion of Christ, in the vital presence of his Spirit. Death and sin continue, but they do not rule us anymore.

At the risk of sounding repetitious, let me note that this is, again, a load-bearing point of Paul's account of Christian moral identity. What he does *not* do is offer a program for moral development and Christian growth. He does not say anything to indicate that a set of accepted practices will ensure that we maximize our potential and grow as we should. The conviction that the realization of Christian moral identity can be accomplished programmatically can be held only when that identity is seen as a property of the believer rather than as a property of Christ, who is present in the believer. To recall the words of Paul to the Galatians: "Having begun with the Spirit, are you now trying to finish with the flesh?" (3:3, my trans.). At the crucial load-bearing points of his moral account, Paul does not point readers to a program of development, even of the kind represented diffusely in classical texts that speak of virtue, but points them back to the baptism that expresses their identification with and in Christ.

1 Corinthians 10:2 and 12:13: Unity in Christ and the Oneness of God

When we turn to the baptism texts in 1 Corinthians, which we will consider much more briefly, two things are striking. First, Paul uses the language of baptism in 1 Cor. 10 in connection with the story of the exodus and in a way that suggests that the Israelites enjoyed a proleptic experience of the gospel itself:

> For I do not want you to be unaware, brothers, that our fathers were all under the cloud, and all passed through the sea, and all were baptized into Moses in the cloud and in the sea, and all ate the same spiritual food, and all drank the same spiritual drink. For they drank from the spiritual Rock that followed them, and the Rock was Christ. (1 Cor. 10:1–4)

As I have argued elsewhere,[5] Paul's logic in the wider passage requires that the experience of Israel was truly *evangelical*, gospel-shaped. It can therefore serve as a warning about the dangers of idolatry for Spirit-filled Christians: if those who drank from the spiritual rock of Christ in the past can be led into idolatry, so can we. Without getting tied up in how being baptized "into Moses" might relate to being baptized "into Christ,"[6] it is defensible to say that Paul now thinks about Israel's moral identity differently, through the prism of the mystery revealed in Christ. When Israel truly enjoyed fellowship with God in the law and covenant, it was because they were fed by Christ and his Spirit. As such, their own transformation of identity was also rendered in a baptism of sorts, as they passed from one reality into another. The law came to them not as a thing in itself but as something belonging to this larger reality. Paul, in other words, cannot now help thinking sacramentally about the story of Israel, because the sacraments are such central articulations of the gospel.

It is striking, then, that Paul uses this language in the context of a passage that will build toward a discussion of the Lord's Supper, which we will consider further in chapter 4. That table itself is mentioned in 10:21 as something that must not be compromised by attendance at the table of idols, which would probably have been common social practice in Corinth. The bread consumed at the table is mentioned a few verses earlier, in 10:17, where the key thing stressed about the loaf is its oneness: "Because there is one bread, we who are many are one body, for we all partake of the one bread."

This is important, because the next occurrence of baptism language is found in the context of Paul's description of the body of Christ in 1 Cor. 12, which is preceded by his more extensive teaching on the Lord's Supper in 1 Cor. 11, where "the body of Christ"

5. See my "Incarnational Ontology and the Theology of Participation in Paul."
6. The expression, I think, is intended to indicate that a qualitative difference remains between those whose earthly, time-bound mediator and covenant representative was Moses and those whose mediator is Christ. The "mystery" language that Paul uses elsewhere (e.g., in Col. 1:25–27) suggests that Christ was always the true covenant mediator, his temporal ministry taken into the eternal dealings of God and determining all of God's relationship to the cosmos and to the sinners who inhabit it. For a time, though, the relationship was subject to a further level of mediation through Moses and the law, an interpretation in line with Paul's language in Gal. 3:23–26.

is core to the symbolism. Baptism and Eucharist are thus mutually informative for the apostle: "For just as the body is one and has many members, and all the members of the body, though many, are one body, so it is with Christ. For in one Spirit we were all baptized into one body—Jews or Greeks, slaves or free—and all were made to drink of one Spirit" (1 Cor. 12:12–13). We should be attentive to the principal emphasis here on unity within diversity. We have come full circle, for the same issues were highlighted in the context of Gal. 3:26. Note that Paul does not say, "As it is with members of the body, so it is with Christians: we all form a single entity in our fellowship." Rather, he says, "So it is with Christ." So the body is represented as having a singular identity that is associated with *his* prior singular identity. The oneness of the body is not something that we work to achieve by the quality of our fellowship but something that we work to manifest in our realization of the singular identity (Jesus) who unites us. This is the very same point that is made of the Spirit in 12:12–13: "In one Spirit we were all baptized into one body, . . . and all were made to drink of one Spirit."[7]

The repetition of the word "one" here is important. It echoes the language of oneness used in 1 Cor. 8:6, which itself draws on the Shema of Deut. 6:4 ("Hear, O Israel: The LORD our God, the LORD is one"):

> For although there may be so-called gods in heaven or on earth—as indeed there are many "gods" and many "lords"—yet for us there is one God, the Father, from whom are all things and for whom we exist, and one Lord, Jesus Christ, through whom are all things and through whom we exist. (1 Cor. 8:5–6)

Here Paul emphasizes that Christian unity is a function not of our reciprocity but of the prior oneness of God. As Paul will say more explicitly in Eph. 4:5, there is "one Lord, one faith, one baptism." This is important because, at a popular level, evangelicals have widely bought into the idea known as social trinitarianism.[8] The simplest

7. In what follows, I am indebted to my doctoral student Kris Song, at the University of Aberdeen, who is researching the unitive role of the Spirit in Paul's thought.

8. The popularity of the view has extended into academic biblical studies, which has functionally separated from the study of theology. When biblical scholars do turn to theology, they often do so without adequate context, drawn to approaches like

way to describe this position is that it sees the oneness of God as
emerging from his threeness by the perfection of fellowship as a
dynamic trinitarian "dance." This departs from the classical way
of thinking of trinitarianism as beginning with the singularity and
simplicity of God. Paul, though, continually reasserts the traditional
monotheistic claim that God is one, albeit now in a trinitarian register, and represents the oneness of God as the basis of Christian
oneness.

We must allow ourselves to feel the force of this. We frequently
approach Christian unity as something that follows from what we
are or what we do: we see Christian unity as constituted by doctrinal agreement or by moral alignment. We consider there to be no
meaningful unity between someone who takes a different position on
this or that doctrinal issue or this or that moral position. The way
we approach evangelical ethics often reflects this. Even if we have
a good emphasis on unity, it is often understood as an imperative
modeled on Jesus's willingness to love the other,[9] which still needs
to move toward agreement by dialogue. But proper reflection on the
sacraments confounds this: for Paul, our unity is a function of our
union with Christ, which is a union with the one God, whose oneness
becomes ours. Our attempts to draw a circle around those who think
like us is fundamentally wrongheaded and, frankly, sinful. Now, this is
not to say that it is wrong to pursue moral and theological agreement
in the truth; it is important to do so, but we do it to bring the high-
est glory to God, not to define who is in and who is out. I am united
to the believer whose doctrine is dreadful and to the one whose life
I find abhorrent; it is precisely because they share in the oneness of

---

social trinitarianism because they are unaware of the reasons classical trinitarianism
took the shape that it did. Katherine Sonderegger's excellent *Doctrine of God* does
a good job of recognizing that prioritizing the oneness of God is simply a matter of
observing the shape of the biblical witness. We can approach the incipient trinitarian theology of the NT only *through* the Shema and the monotheistic assertions
of, e.g., Isaiah. For a thorough critical evaluation of social trinitarianism, see Kilby,
"Perichoresis and Projection."

9. This seems to me to be a deficiency reflected in Burridge, *Imitating Jesus*. While
there is much to appreciate in this book, it focuses too narrowly on emulating the
values represented in the Gospel narratives and is not attentive to the grounding of
much of Paul's ethics in the nature of God himself.

Christ's body that I am compelled to speak to both problems, but to do so in brotherly love and affirmation. For Paul, the sine qua non of inclusion seems to be limited to the confession "Jesus is Lord," which can be made only by the acting presence of the Spirit (1 Cor. 12:3).[10]

Conclusion

My purpose in this chapter has been to draw the reader's attention to the prominence that baptism has within Paul's account of Christian moral identity. At key load-bearing points he directs his audience to consider the significance of their baptism as a ritual that enacts their union with Christ and that speaks to their moral identity. Their moral practice must emerge from this.

The first key observation is that Paul considers baptism to signify the clothing of oneself with Christ. This is an observation that we will unpack further in chapter 5, where we will consider how the use of clothing imagery is developed in relation to the ongoing process of mortification as we strive actively to put sin to death. Here the point is simple: baptism signifies that the Christian life involves donning the identity of someone else and not simply improving our own. What we clothe ourselves with is not a new set of attitudes or practices but another person, Jesus Christ. If anything else is substituted for him at that load-bearing point of our moral account, then everything else will collapse. For if we put anything else there, it will serve only our instinct for idolatry, and we will find ourselves enslaved again to the "elemental principles of the world."

The second observation is that because baptism signifies clothing ourselves with the same perfections of Christ by which we are justified, it actually intensifies the challenge of sanctification rather than softening it. For any of us to sin is fundamentally at odds with our new identity, since it is fundamentally at odds with *his* identity. This speaks at once to two different problems in the interpretation

10. I want to acknowledge the importance of my teacher in systematic theology at the Free Church of Scotland College, Donald Macleod, who stressed this point repeatedly in our classes. Much of my subsequent interest in union with Christ as a theme goes back to his emphasis on it in the classroom. The day when he made this point about Christian unity was a "lightbulb" moment for me.

or application of Paul's teaching. First, it speaks to the movements in NT scholarship and modern theology, such as the apocalyptic Paul, that minimize the importance of the Christian's moral activity in favor of the divine invasion of grace. Such a position simply cannot accommodate the way that Paul represents the moral life of the Christian in relation to baptism. Second, it speaks to the tendency to downplay the true awfulness of our failures by locating them in a narrative of gradual progress toward perfection. This is not to deny the truth that we will continue to experience the war of flesh and Spirit until we are raised with the spiritual bodies of the resurrection and that within this struggle we take comfort from the fact that the righteousness by which we are justified is not our own. Instead, it affirms that when we do fail, our failures involve the true atrocity of living *against* the one who lives in us. They are all the worse because they involve a kind of denial of who we really are.

The third observation is that baptism always carries with it an affirmation of our collective identification with Christ. I am clothed with Christ, but I am not the only one who is so clothed. As many as are baptized into him are clothed with him. Baptism demands that we see our identity as Christians in terms of our participation in the body, the church, and refuses to allow us to define that body in terms of intellectual agreement. Morally, then, any Christian who does not recognize their obligations to affirm the status of others who are clothed with Christ lives at odds with their identity. In fact, they live at odds with the identity of God himself, since the oneness of the church is a function of the oneness of the God to whom we are united in Christ. The moral identity of those who are baptized into Christ, then, must be characterized by love.

4

The Lord's Supper
and Someone Else's Memory

Do This in Remembrance of Me

Our identities are very closely linked to our memories. *Who we are* is shaped by *what we remember* because our identity is, in part at least, narratival, and our memories constitute our story. In the modern world, we tend to think about memories as the properties of individuals, created by neural states recollecting things that happened to them in their pasts. This identifies the neural condition of memory with the identity of the individual. "What I remember" is essential to "who I am."

In contrast to this individualist notion of memory, we sometimes use the language of "remembrance" in relation to collective activities—remembering the fallen in war, for example—and in doing so we shift to what is really an entirely different definition of "remembering." Here we remember what happened to someone else: we honor someone else's story without conflating it with our own. The concept of memory at work here is definitively different and one that does not intrude on our sense of personal identity.

This chapter will probe the way in which Paul represents the Lord's Supper as an act of remembrance, not merely in the sense that we honor what happened to someone else, but in the sense that we consider the memory of his story to be the memory of our story. In other words, we bridge the two categories of memory that I mentioned above, with all the implications for identity that this entails: what we remember in this dramatic rite defines who we understand ourselves to be. The Lord's Supper is a dramatic performance of someone else's memory by which we make their past our own and, as we do so, make their future our own. Something similar could be said about baptism, which we discussed in the previous chapter and which also plays a key role in defining Christian identity, but it is the Lord's Supper that is distinctively represented in terms of memory or remembrance. The "someone else" here is Jesus, and the driving point in this chapter is that if *our* moral identity is constituted by *his*, then the sacraments are key means of grace by which this identity is formed. We perform memories of what is now considered to be *our* story and hence inhabit our new identities. As we shall see, a central element of performance is carried over from the dramatic identification made during the celebration of Passover.

This is difficult for us to comprehend as moderns, since we work with the kind of assumptions about how memory and identity are related that I outlined above. Before we turn to consider the biblical material, then, I want to probe this relationship a little further by reflecting on how it is represented in the critically acclaimed *Blade Runner* movies and analyzing these in dialogue with the work of John Swinton on time, memory, and community.

What Am I to You? Memory, Identity, and Relationship

Both of the *Blade Runner* movies—the original from 1982 and the recently released sequel, *Blade Runner 2049*—are preoccupied with the relationship between memory and identity.[1] For those who have not seen the movies, the premise is that there are synthetic humans,

---

1. The first movie was loosely adapted from a novel by Philip K. Dick, *Do Androids Dream of Electric Sheep?*, though many of the key elements, including the

androids known as "replicants," some of which have had memories implanted into them to provide a framework for emotional and psychological experience in order to buffer their potentially destructive abilities. These memories may belong to someone else, or they may have been artificially generated. In the original film, one character is unaware that this has been done to her: she believes that she is the person whose childhood she remembers, and she has no knowledge of the fact that she is actually a recently manufactured android. In the sequel, much of the story revolves around the question of whether a particular memory in the mind of the central character is real and whether it is really his. Both films probe the way that memories shape our identity. In very open-ended ways, both ask what significance should be attached to a memory that may not actually be associated with something physically experienced by the one who remembers it. Do I cease to be myself just because that particular memory didn't happen to me? Am I, in a positive way, a particular kind of person with a particular set of relationships because of a memory that recollects something that actually happened to someone else? A crucial, and beautifully understated, moment in the second movie has Harrison Ford's Deckard asking a replicant, "What am I to you?" The viewer knows that, because of a particular implanted memory, he is nothing less than "father" to that replicant. The viewer also knows that, because others have the same memory, this fatherly relationship extends beyond this one individual—and beyond the person whose true memory it is—to a whole family.

What makes these films effective, the reason they have had such enduring appeal to audiences (the original, at least, has had a great impact, and the sequel is widely regarded as a "future classic"), is that they open up a set of issues about the relationship between memory and identity that we often process through a set of very modern assumptions. We consider memories to be a property of the individual, inhering in a neural state that has been generated by the experiences of our bodies and contributing to our identity in a way that is vulnerable to the compromise of that neural state. Dementia, for example, is

---

title *Blade Runner* and the ambiguity over the central character's identity, are not found in the book.

frightening because those whose memories are compromised appear to be losing themselves or to be lost to those around them.

My colleague John Swinton highlights that it is precisely the individualistic way of thinking about both memory and identity that makes this fate so disturbing to moderns. It is not just that we conceive of memory in relation to the individual person, but we conceive of the person's personhood in relation to their memories. Swinton seeks to reorient the concept of memory and identity toward social and relational accounts of a kind that is more visible outside the modern West. In this view, one whose personal memories are compromised is not lost, because the fellowship around that person sustains the memories that their own mind cannot.[2] A "social memory" is at work, not necessarily of the sort that some have applied to the transmission of the Gospel stories,[3] but one in which the memories of the person and the attendant storied identity are sustained through the community. Who that person is does not, in the end, depend on the reliability of their neurochemistry. This is a particular element of what is sometimes described today as "embodied cognition," a term expressing the idea that our cognitive processing of the world is not confined to the activity of our brains but involves the whole body in which that brain exists and the communities in which that body exists socially. All of this seeks to correct a particular kind of individualism in the way we conceive of cognition, including the processing of memories. Modernity continues to feel the reverberations of Descartes's *cogito*, which we might modify for present purposes: "I remember, therefore I am."

Our way of thinking about the relationship between memory and identity is also shaped by a way of thinking about time. Time is a series of events, moving from the past to the future. My identity is formed out of my past, as I remember it, out of the events that affected me or in which I participated. My identity may have a different shape in the future, *following* another series of events that will themselves become part of my past (just a more recent part).

Taken together, these ways of thinking about memory as something linked to the identity of the individual affect the way we think

2. Swinton, *Dementia.*

3. See the overview by Chris Keith, "Social Memory Theory and Gospels Research."

about acts of commemoration. Here we tend to use the language of "remembering" as if we have moved into a different dictionary entry, one associated with showing respect to the experience of someone else. In the UK, for example, we hold a Remembrance Day that commemorates the end of the First World War, though it is also associated with subsequent conflicts. When we use the language of remembrance here, we mean that we are remembering what happened to someone else: it may have affected me in some way—I do not live under German rule—but it is essentially an act of remembering someone else's story. It has to be, because I was not there.

Now, it may seem that I am confusing two different concepts of memory. In contrast to *Blade Runner*, the memory in question is not a neural state that corresponds to a subjective experience. Part of my point, though, is that we have *reduced* the concept of memory to the neurophysical phenomena that take place within an individual, and specifically within the individual's brain. For the most part, in the modern world, we no longer have space for the kind of social memory that Swinton speaks of, which is an embodied and communal reality, represented as much (and as truly) in the spoken or performative testimony of members of the community as it is in the neural state associated with the sensory experience of a moment in history. Social memory can be testimonial, and that testimony can be transmitted for millennia without losing its significance.

Memory and Ritual Identification in Judaism

Before we look at Paul's treatments of the Eucharist, I want to consider some important background to this concept of identification by *performative memory* found in the Jewish ritual and festal traditions, particularly Passover. Along with other feasts, Passover functions as an act of what we might call "participatory commemoration." This selection of verses from the Exodus account highlights such identification:

> This day shall be for you a memorial day, and you shall keep it as a feast to the LORD; throughout your generations, as a statute forever, you shall keep it as a feast. . . . And you shall observe the Feast of

Unleavened Bread, for on this very day I brought your hosts out of the land of Egypt. Therefore you shall observe this day, throughout your generations, as a statute forever. . . . You shall observe this rite as a statute for you and for your sons forever. And when you come to the land that the LORD will give you, as he has promised, you shall keep this service. And when your children say to you, "What do you mean by this service?" you shall say, "It is the sacrifice of the LORD's Passover, for he passed over the houses of the people of Israel in Egypt, when he struck the Egyptians but spared our houses." (12:14, 17, 24–27)

Unleavened bread shall be eaten for seven days; no leavened bread shall be seen with you, and no leaven shall be seen with you in all your territory. *You shall tell your son on that day, "It is because of what the LORD did for me when I came out of Egypt."* And it shall be to you *as a sign on your hand and as a memorial between your eyes*, that the law of the LORD may be in your mouth. For with a strong hand the LORD has brought you out of Egypt. You shall therefore keep this statute at its appointed time from year to year. (13:7–10, emphasis added)

A key point here is that while the address within the narrative is directed toward the participants in the actual exodus, who can straightforwardly use the first-person expression "what the LORD did for me" (13:8), this institutes a form of words that will be recited by those not themselves present in this generation, who will also speak these words to their children. The point is highlighted in later Jewish seder traditions, which are contained in the Passover Haggadah and may possibly reflect the customs of the NT period.[4] There, the one presiding (the father) is expected to recite verses from Deut. 26:5–9, which are not properly about Passover but are linked into the feast and stress the element of identification:

4. The point is debated, but see my brief discussion in *Union with Christ*, 201–16. P. Markus Nikkanen has recently made a robust defense of the claim that the Passover meal in the Second Temple period shared many elements with the later seder and was inalienably participatory in character, something that can be traced back to the exodus account itself. His doctoral dissertation, "Participation in Christ: Paul and Pre-Pauline Eucharistic Tradition," was accepted by the University of Aberdeen in 2018 and will, I hope, be published soon.

And you shall make response before the LORD your God, "A wandering Aramean was *my* father. And he went down into Egypt and sojourned there, few in number, and there he became a nation, great, mighty, and populous. And the Egyptians treated *us* harshly and humiliated *us* and laid on *us* hard labor. Then *we* cried to the LORD, the God of our fathers, and the LORD heard *our* voice and saw *our* affliction, *our* toil, and *our* oppression. And the LORD brought *us* out of Egypt with a mighty hand and an outstretched arm, with great deeds of terror, with signs and wonders. And he brought *us* into this place and gave *us* this land, a land flowing with milk and honey." (26:5–9, emphasis added)

All of this leads to a thorough sense of identification. This dramatic reenactment of that first Passover is done in such a way as to say, "This is *my* story." What is crucial about this is the relational definition that it generates. It defines my relationship with God, my relationship with the rest of the nation, my relationship with Egypt as an emblem of a moral world from which I am delivered, and my relationship to the land, whether I am in it or exiled from it. These are not someone else's relationships; they are mine. And I live in a different way because of them.

This way of thinking about acts of commemoration is largely alien to us today, though scholars working in the social sciences will be quick to point out that our modern, Western notion of memory is the real oddity. Look to the past, or look to societies outside the modern West (perhaps, even, outside the *urban* West), and you find those whose concept of time and memory allows a much richer sense of identification with those whose memories are recalled in commemorative acts. Within the biblical material, the concept that underpins this is covenant: there is a formal union between God and his people that binds him to them and them to one another, and their stories are shared through this covenant frame. The story of the exodus, within which Passover takes place, is the story of the covenant. It places its members out of Egypt, heading into the promised land, in fellowship with the one God.

But while affirming the significance of covenant as a conceptual category, it is important to stress that the *imaginative* or *performative* ritual identification inherent in Passover and other feasts needs to be made *actual*, to be *actualized*. A number of passages in the OT indicate the importance of an inner transformation that *realizes* the significance of the performed ritual. For example, a cluster of such texts speak of circumcision in these terms:

> Circumcise therefore the foreskin of your heart, and be no longer stubborn. (Deut. 10:16)

> And the LORD your God will circumcise your heart and the heart of your offspring, so that you will love the LORD your God with all your heart and with all your soul, that you may live. (Deut. 30:6)

> Circumcise yourselves to the LORD;
>   remove the foreskin of your hearts,
>   O men of Judah and inhabitants of Jerusalem;
> lest my wrath go forth like fire,
>   and burn with none to quench it,
>   because of the evil of your deeds. (Jer. 4:4)

Effectively, this is a way of saying that ritual identifications are meaningless if they are *merely* performative; the dramatic ritual must correspond to an internal reality. The narratives of God's people, though, make clear that such an inner moral state is impossible for them to achieve and sustain naturally. Hence, in several key passages, this emphasis on inner transformation turns toward the future and is associated with the need for God himself to change his people, intervening from outside in a future act of deliverance. This becomes the substance of hope for the OT prophets. Famously, Jer. 31:31–34 speaks of the new covenant that God will make, which will include an inner transformation. "For this is the covenant that I will make with the house of Israel after those days, declares the LORD: I will put my law within them, and I will write it on their hearts. And I will be their God, and they shall be my people" (31:33).

Ezekiel, meanwhile, uses similar imagery of transformation but associates it with the language of "spirit":

> And I will give them one heart, and a new spirit I will put within them.
> I will remove the heart of stone from their flesh and give them a heart
> of flesh. (11:19)

> And I will give you a new heart, and a new spirit I will put within you. And I will remove the heart of stone from your flesh and give you a heart of flesh. And I will put my Spirit within you, and cause you to walk in my statutes and be careful to obey my rules. (36:26–27)

These two passages overlap in an important way: both speak of the law (and its constituent decrees) being obeyed through an internal change wrought by God himself. The law is no longer an external standard to which God's people strive to conform but is stamped on their character. The overlapping language of the texts (the words that they share) would allow Jews to read them together, intertextually. The legal dimension does not stand in isolation, though; it is better understood as covenantal rather than legal, for its purpose is to secure the real communion expressed in the words "I will be their God, and they shall be my people" (Jer. 31:33). This is a matter of life and blessing, for God is the source of both. Hence, in the wider context, Ezekiel uses further imagery of God's own Spirit working to bring life. The famous "valley of dry bones" passage in chapter 37 is a striking visual metaphor of the Spirit working to bring life where there is death, to bring hope to what cannot create hope from itself.

I stress all of this because Paul reads these texts of inner transformation together in relation to the new covenant:

> Are we beginning to commend ourselves again? Or do we need, as some do, letters of recommendation to you, or from you? You yourselves are our letter of recommendation, written on our hearts, to be known and read by all. And you show that you are a letter from Christ delivered by us, written not with ink but with the Spirit of the living God, not on tablets of stone but on tablets of human hearts.
>
> Such is the confidence that we have through Christ toward God. Not that we are sufficient in ourselves to claim anything as coming from us, but our sufficiency is from God, who has made us sufficient to be ministers of a new covenant, not of the letter but of the Spirit. For the letter kills, but the Spirit gives life. (2 Cor. 3:1–6)

Paul here, quite strikingly, describes the new covenant as one "not of the letter but of the Spirit": the new covenant is, characteristically, the covenant of the Spirit. We can see here elements from Jer. 31

and elements from Ezek. 36 and 37 read together as describing the same thing. The imagery of the divine law and commands written on hearts is now recast in terms of Christ's letter imprinted on our inner being; the mode of relationship to such standards is, therefore, different. They are not external requirements by which, if carried out, we acquire capital but characteristics linked to Christ himself. I am someone in whom God's law has been inscribed; it is not something I perform to acquire currency with him, or with people around me, but something I embody.

The Lord's Supper

Turning now to the Lord's Supper, we see that we are firmly in the territory of memory: "Do this in remembrance of me" (1 Cor. 11:24). Paul represents this memory as something that is passed on: "I received from the Lord what I also passed on to you" (11:23, my trans.), which highlights something of the traditional and testimonial character of Christian faith. A memory has been shared with us by centuries of Christian practice. We access that memory only through the agency of others. We remember the head through the ministry of the body, and this contributes to our sense of identity. It leaves no space for an individualistic account of the Christian life. My very knowledge of Jesus has been brokered through the body.

Paul's teaching on the Lord's Supper in 1 Cor. 11 understands the sacrament to recollect formally the last meal of Jesus and his disciples, and it presents the elements of the meal as rendering the true significance of Jesus's death. Some scholarship has argued that this connection is a late one, imposed on a widespread and diverse early Christian culture of celebratory banquets, which only eventually became associated with the celebration of the death of Jesus.[5] But the vast majority of scholars consider the link to be authentic and early. The link between the Last Supper and Jesus's death is interesting

---

5. Probably the best-known proponent of this view is Crossan, *Historical Jesus*, 360–67. Less well known, but more thoroughly influential, is Lietzmann, *Mass and Lord's Supper*. For a critical evaluation of the most recent literature on this approach, see Nikkanen, "Participation in Christ."

not least because the Last Supper is itself closely associated with Passover. In the Synoptic Gospels, the Last Supper is represented as a Passover meal, which may have looked quite like a contemporary Jewish seder, depending on how far back those traditions can be traced. In John's Gospel, the timing of the final meal appears to be slightly different; it happens ahead of Passover, so that the death of Jesus is represented as taking place at the point in time when the Passover lambs are killed. There are various ways to explain the differences between these accounts and to reconcile the details, which we will not explore here. Rather, we simply note that, in different ways, both the Synoptics and John explicitly connect the meaning of Passover to the death of Jesus.

As discussed above, Passover is a feast that involves a dramatic identification with the events of the original Passover in such a way that the celebrant says, "This is *my* story." The Synoptics report Jesus as taking the elements of that dramatic reenactment and reinterpreting them as witnesses to the significance of his death. The shortest description is the one in Mark:

> And as they were eating, he took bread, and after blessing it broke it and gave it to them, and said, "Take; this is my body." And he took a cup, and when he had given thanks he gave it to them, and they all drank of it. And he said to them, "This is my blood of the covenant, which is poured out for many. Truly, I say to you, I will not drink again of the fruit of the vine until that day when I drink it new in the kingdom of God." (14:22–25)

Matthew's account is almost identical, except that the words "for the forgiveness of sins" are attached to the description of the blood as poured out for many (26:28). Luke's account, which is most like Paul's, is slightly different still: the body is described as "given for you" (22:19), and the cup is described as "the new covenant in my blood" (22:20).

Again, there is a larger discussion about how these differences might be accounted for. Theologically, what is more important for us is the way that the Gospels, considered alongside one another in the canon, evoke (or invoke) a range of OT passages that contribute to our growing understanding of the significance of the Supper. The

Markan and Matthean expression "blood of the covenant" corresponds word for word to the language used in Exod. 24:8: "And Moses
took the blood and threw it on the people and said, 'Behold the blood
of the covenant that the LORD has made with you in accordance with
all these words.'" This is interesting because we are not here talking
about the blood of a Passover lamb, nor of the animal offered in a
sin or guilt sacrifice; the words describe very specifically the blood
of the unique sacrifice associated with the institution of the Mosaic
covenant. The role of the blood in that ceremony was properly one
of sanctification and ratification: it marked those on whom it was
sprinkled as set apart for relationship with the Holy God, and it
sealed the agreement between the parties.

The Lukan and Pauline version of the words, meanwhile, invokes
the promise of the new covenant that is found in Jer. 31:31–34, which
we have already mentioned as one of the passages that speak of the
necessity of inner transformation:

> Behold, the days are coming, declares the LORD, when I will make *a*
> *new covenant* with the house of Israel and the house of Judah, not
> like the covenant that I made with their fathers on the day when I took
> them by the hand to bring them out of the land of Egypt, my covenant
> that they broke, though I was their husband, declares the LORD. For
> this is the covenant that I will make with the house of Israel after
> those days, declares the LORD: I will put my law within them, and I
> will write it on their hearts. And I will be their God, and they shall
> be my people. And no longer shall each one teach his neighbor and
> each his brother, saying, "Know the LORD," for they shall all know
> me, from the least of them to the greatest, declares the LORD. For I
> will forgive their iniquity, and I will remember their sin no more. (Jer.
> 31:31–34, emphasis added)

We are dealing, then, with a set of allusions that creates both correspondences and distinctions between covenants: life in the eucharistic community is at once like and unlike life under the old
covenant. The story of Moses and the exodus is now relativized
with respect to the story of the death of Jesus, whose blood is the
true blood of the covenant that is unlike the covenant that has been
broken. As an act of memory, the Lord's Supper invites us to share

the memory not only of Jesus but of Jesus and his disciples in communion. They eat a meal that involves a collective, performative identification with the experiences of the exodus generation, and Jesus then *re-identifies* the significance of the elements with his death. We remember, specifically, him ("Do this in remembrance of me"), but we do so in a drama that casts us with the disciples as the twelve tribes who feast with their mediator and draw their life from him.

Two things stand out in the Jeremiah quotation, especially when considered in the light of what we have seen throughout this study. The first is the emphasis on an alien reality being inserted into us with transformational effects: *I* will write *my* law on *their* hearts. The second, a corollary of this, is the impact that this change has on the commodity value of righteousness and knowledge: "No longer shall each one teach his neighbor and each his brother, saying, 'Know the LORD,' for they shall all know me, from the least of them to the greatest, declares the LORD" (31:34a). Understood in relation to Jeremiah's prophecy—as the Last Supper narrative demands that it must be—the new covenant refuses all attempts to possess status within the community on the basis of a perceived capital of knowledge or righteousness: all, equally, know the Lord and enjoy forgiveness. As we will see, that is particularly interesting in the context of 1 Cor. 11.

Before we turn to consider 1 Cor. 11, let me mention one more background text. Luke's account, echoed in Paul's, specifies that the body represented by the bread is "given for you" (Luke 22:19). Paul drops the word "given" and simply has "for you," or as we might translate it, "on your behalf" (1 Cor. 11:24). The word translated "given" is *didōmi* (Luke 22:19), a Greek word that lies at the root of several others: when a prefix is attached, it takes on a particular meaning or acquires a certain subtlety. While Paul's description of the Supper drops that word, 1 Cor. 11:23 contains two striking examples of the prefixed form *paradidōmi*, which appears in the expression "on the night when he was betrayed" (*en tē nykti hē paredideto*) and when Paul speaks of passing on the tradition he has received (*ho kai paredōka hymin*). Although it might sound like we are pressing the significance of one word too hard, a number of scholars have seen the repetition of *paradidōmi* to echo its use in the Greek version of Isa. 53:6, 12:[6]

> All we as sheep have gone astray; every one has gone astray in his way; and the Lord delivered him up [*paredōken*, handed him over] for our sins [cf. Heb. "has laid on him the iniquity of us all"]. . . . Therefore he shall inherit many, and he shall divide the spoils of the mighty; because his soul was delivered [*paredothē*, "handed over"; cf. Heb. "he poured himself out"] to death: and he was numbered among the transgressors; and he bore the sins of many, and was delivered [*paredothē*, handed over; cf. Heb. "he made intercession"] because of their iniquities.[7]

The frequency with which the word is used within a relatively short range of verses suggests that 1 Cor. 11:23 is indeed alluding to Isa. 53, but the significant point is that the language repeatedly refers to some act of substitution, however conceived.

So, what we have in 1 Cor. 11 is Paul's application of the Lord's Supper to the moral identity of the Corinthian church: it is an act that performs a memory of what Jesus has done in fellowship with his covenant nation of twelve disciples. Jesus's action is itself understood in relation to the paradigmatic covenant memory of the exodus, in which the distinctive relationship of Israel to God and to the world is manifest. This is now reconfigured in relation to his act of representation, by which we are delivered from iniquity and its consequences. It strips us of any notion of having a capital of our own before God and instead sets us as beneficiaries of Christ, participating in his goodness.

Before I probe the ethical load that this carries in Paul's argument in 1 Corinthians, I want to make an important observation that is broadly true of Paul's ethical teaching, not just of what he says concerning the Lord's Supper. Paul consistently points to what the church is in Christ as the grounds for how it should live, rather than pointing to what it might be if it will only get its moral act together.

6. On these allusions, see Hays, *First Corinthians*, 198.
7. Lancelot Brenton, *The Septuagint with Apocrypha in English* (London: Samuel & Bagster, 1851), with my annotations.

Consistently, he says, "This is what you are, so start to live accordingly, because right now you are monstrously inconsistent with it." The logic is not so much that we have not yet fulfilled our potential but is actually much more scathing: we are doing violence to our identity in Christ with our moral failings.

Holiness and Separateness

What part does the Lord's Supper play in Paul's ethical teaching, then? First of all, it articulates the holiness of participants as sharers in the identity of Jesus and the basic incompatibility of that holiness with participation in idolatry: you are not in Egypt or in Babylon; you are in Christ. I used a lot of "participation" words there quite deliberately. In 1 Cor. 10, Paul leads his readers back to the story of the wilderness wanderings of Israel after the exodus, presenting them as a people who have drunk from the rock of Christ—that is, as people who have experienced the blessing of the gospel in some sense—and yet are still vulnerable to the danger of idolatry. Similarly, those in the church today who have drunk from Christ are vulnerable to the lures of idols. As the chapter progresses, Paul speaks of the cup and the bread as means of "sharing" in the body and blood of Jesus (10:16, my trans.). The word he uses is the well-known term *koinōnia*, which can mean fellowship, but in which there is an acknowledgment of correspondence or identification between members: something is common to all of them. In the next verse, he uses a different word, the verb *metechō*, to speak of our partaking of the one bread, by which many are made one. I'll come back to the theme of unity in a moment, but here I want to note the parallel that Paul then draws between those who partake in the Lord's Supper, at the Lord's Table, and Israel's relationship to the altar:

> Consider the people of Israel: are not those who eat the sacrifices participants in the altar? What do I imply then? That food offered to idols is anything, or that an idol is anything? No, I imply that what pagans sacrifice they offer to demons and not to God. I do not want you to be participants with demons. (1 Cor. 10:18–20)

This passage is interesting because Paul is seeking both to nullify any perception that idols have substance or significance and to warn Christians not to take part in idol feasts. He is aware of the danger that properly considering idols to be empty of real divinity can lead to the view that being present at an idol feast is a matter of indifference, a nonissue. He responds to this by stressing that there is always a participation at work: if you sit at the table of a demon (even if that demon is just a fiction), you are participating in the identity of that demon, participating in everything that the demon represents and stands for in the mythos of its worshipers. If you sit at the table of the Lord, you participate in his identity and all that it stands for. You cannot participate in both identities, because they are incompatible.

This way of thinking about moral decision making is quite different from the kind of command-obedience model that we often use: it takes us down to the very fundamentals of how our participation in the identity of Jesus, performed in the sacrament of the Lord's Supper, positions us with respect to the world. Just as Israel's participation in the altar constantly enacted a monotheistic identity that recognized the jealousy necessary to a covenantal relationship with the one God, so our participation in the Lord's Supper enacts or performs a jealously monotheistic identity.

A similar logic is at work further back in the letter, in Paul's teaching on sexual morality in chapters 5 and 6. These are not obviously passages in which Paul is thinking about the Lord's Supper, but even here there are hints that he is thinking eucharistically about Christian ethics.[8] In chapter 6 he writes:

> Do you not know that your bodies are members of Christ? Shall I then take the members of Christ and make them members of a prostitute? Never! Or do you not know that he who is joined to a prostitute becomes one body with her? For, as it is written, "The two will become one flesh." But he who is joined to the Lord becomes one spirit with him. (1 Cor. 6:15–17)

---

8. I am indebted to Markus Nikkanen, whose work I have cited several times, for highlighting the extent to which Paul's ethics in chap. 5 are shaped by covenantal notions of purity and very specifically the connections between these and Passover.

Note the similarity of this language with chapter 10 and with the description of the body in chapter 12, straight after the Eucharist account of chapter 11. Membership of the body is not a symbol here but a reality. Immediately after this, Paul speaks of the body as the temple of the Holy Spirit, which is a statement that designates the believer as a sacred space, a holy entity that should not be defiled by any uncleanness; the problem with sexual immorality is precisely that it is incompatible with the holiness associated with the believer in union with Christ. It actively defiles the sacred.

Interestingly, the emphasis on purity here is anticipated in 1 Cor. 5:6–8 by the reappropriation of Passover imagery in connection with the sacrifice of Jesus:

> Your boasting is not good. Do you not know that a little leaven leavens the whole lump? Cleanse out the old leaven that you may be a new lump, as you really are unleavened. For Christ, our Passover lamb, has been sacrificed. Let us therefore celebrate the festival, not with the old leaven, the leaven of malice and evil, but with the unleavened bread of sincerity and truth. (1 Cor. 5:6–8)

The boasting here specifically concerns sexual morality, so we are really in the same unit of thought as in chapter 6. The imagery of purity that Paul uses is of preparation for the Passover meal: the house (indeed, the whole community) is to be rid of leaven, the presence of which will fundamentally compromise the holiness of the celebration. In this connection, Paul points to the new identity of those in the community: they are to clean out the old yeast so that they may be a new batch (not a new batch of yeast, but a new batch of bread, a new loaf). However, even this statement of purpose concerns realizing what the community already actually is: "as you really are unleavened" (5:7). He goes on to identify Christ as the paschal lamb and to urge the community to celebrate the festival properly, with the new bread and not the old yeast. So even in chapter 5—some chapters removed from the discussions of the Lord's Supper in chapter 10 and in chapter 11—Paul thinks about the morality of the Christian life, specifically, the morality of sexual life, in terms that are informed particularly by the Lord's Supper.

It is striking, moreover, that of all the places in the OT to which he could have pointed the Corinthians to shape their thinking about sexual morality, he does not direct them to the obvious places that we might go—Gen. 1 and 2, perhaps, or the laws about sex in the Pentateuch—but to the Passover preparations. The law is perhaps assumed as the standard that defines proper and improper conduct, but the Passover imagery redefined through the Lord's Supper provides the fundamental basis for Paul's instruction. He takes the Corinthians back to the most basic issues of identity, and identity understood ontologically, in terms of *what they are*: you *are* in a symbolic but real sense unleavened, and you are so because you are united to Christ, so cleanse yourself of the old yeast that clings to you.

For those of us who may be involved in the discipleship of other Christians—and in some respects that is all of us—this particular characteristic of Paul's moral teaching is vitally important. Paul never allows moral issues to be considered in isolation from our identity in Christ. He never allows them to become issues in their own right, things we can do or activities we can perform in order to be considered as conforming to a standard. His use of eucharistic imagery takes us back to the basis of the goodness manifest within the believer and the believing community, the personal presence of Christ. "I no longer live, but Christ lives in me"; I am holy, because he is holy. It is important for us to ask whether we employ a similar strategy or whether—unlike Paul and rather more like the Pharisees and the circumcision party—we start with the issues, with definitions of Christian ethical positions, and don't stress at each and every turn that these will themselves become matters of idolatry if approached apart from our union with Christ.

Oneness

As well as speaking to the purity of the community, the Lord's Supper speaks to the practice of unity within it. Even in the verses that we have just considered, which are principally about sexual purity, Paul has used language that demands the practicing of love and peace (see 1 Cor. 5:8 and 6:15–17, quoted above). Paul's statement in 1 Cor. 6:15–17, in particular, anticipates much of the language that Paul will use in 1 Cor. 10, 11, and 12 concerning Christian unity: we are members of Christ and the one Spirit that we share with him, so we also share with one another in Christ. So while in chapter 6, Paul's teaching on union with Christ bears on sexual morality; in chapters 10–12, that very same language bears on unity and peace.

The word "one" becomes something of a motif throughout chapters 10–12:

> Because there is one bread, we who are many are one body, for we all partake of the one bread. (10:17)

> For in one Spirit we were all baptized into one body—Jews or Greeks, slaves or free—and all were made to drink of one Spirit. (12:13)

As we noted in the preceding chapter, Paul's emphasis on oneness is anchored in the oneness of God himself, with the appropriation of the Shema in 1 Cor. 8:6 playing a key role in the development of Paul's thought.

> For although there may be so-called gods in heaven or on earth—as indeed there are many "gods" and many "lords"—yet for us there is one God, the Father, from whom are all things and for whom we exist, and one Lord, Jesus Christ, through whom are all things and through whom we exist. (8:5–6)

God is one, and those united to the one God through the one mediator Jesus by the one Spirit are also, therefore, one. Their unity resides not in moral or doctrinal agreement but in their shared union, symbolized in the elements of the Lord's Supper. There are certainly some questions to be asked about how we relate this to Paul's teaching about shunning those who are immoral, but the core premise of Paul's thinking is clear: we are one because we are united by the Spirit, through the Son, to the one God. To repeat the point that we made in the last chapter, Paul's logic is quite at odds with the kind of social trinitarianism that is often encountered at a popular level in our theology: the unity of the church is not an emulation of a perfected dance of fellowship between three persons but an outflowing of the essential oneness of God.

It would be easy to make some fairly banal observations about this unity, but what I want to draw attention to is how Paul's thinking about eucharistic unity draws together some of the threads that we saw at work in the biblical backgrounds to the Lord's Supper. These move beyond banalities and into the subtle dynamics of how the Lord's Supper counters our instinct to elevate ourselves, to be self-idolaters.

The Lord's Supper is, as we have seen, a covenant meal: the cup signifies Jesus's blood of the covenant and therefore the sanctification of the participants as a holy community set in a special relationship with God. But it is, specifically, a new covenant meal, which understands this community in terms of Jeremiah's expectation that "they shall all know me, from the least of them to the greatest," and "no longer shall each teach . . . his brother" (31:34). Jeremiah's prophecy anticipates a believing community in which the things that normally stratify us into categories of lesser and greater—wealth, wisdom, righteousness—can no longer be commodified in this way. There is no "lesser" and there is no "greater," for everyone will know God. Given that 1 Corinthians opens with a discussion of the factions that have formed around great teachers—"'I follow Apollos,' or 'I follow Cephas'" (1:12)—it is significant that Paul eventually presents the Eucharist in terms of Jeremiah's new covenant. When he castigates those who have formed such factions by asking, "Is Christ divided?" (1:13), he is challenging not simply factions that are opposed because of the doctrinal differences of their teachers—I'm not sure that there was such stark disunity *of that kind*—but rather the problem that these factions are the basis for relativizing the worth of those who belong to them. They are like frat houses on a college campus: the disunity isn't necessarily a matter of conflict between them (though there is some reference to this in the text) but a matter of which are deemed the coolest. Conversely, the expression of true unity is not necessarily about the absence of conflict but about the proper evaluation of those whom we have dismissed as "lesser." So, in 1 Cor. 12, Paul writes:

On the contrary, the parts of the body that seem to be weaker are indispensable, and on those parts of the body that we think less honorable we bestow the greater honor, and our unpresentable parts are treated with greater modesty, which our more presentable parts do not require. But God has so composed the body, giving greater honor to the part that lacked it, that there may be no division in the body, but that the members may have the same care for one another. (12:22–25)

In 1 Cor. 11, the issue is probably more starkly one of economic class: Paul speaks of those who are "have-nots" (*tous mē echontas*, 11:22) being humiliated by others who eat and drink without any care for them. This situation probably reflects the stratification of meals according to the social standing of those present: the have-nots are last to eat, by which time nothing may be left.

For Paul, this is at odds with the true unity of the body as it is represented in the Lord's Supper. All know God, from the least to the greatest; all belong to one body; all have been made to drink of one Spirit, yet some are treated as if they were less than others. The language of the have-nots (*tous mē echontas*) is reminiscent of the "are nots" (*ta mē onta*) that Paul speaks of as the objects of divine election in 1 Cor. 1: "But God chose what is foolish in the world to shame the wise; God chose what is weak in the world to shame the strong; God chose what is low and despised in the world, even things that are not [*ta mē onta*], to bring to nothing things that are, so that no human being might boast in the presence of God" (1:27–29). This is as fundamental a negation of the concept of capital as one can imagine: God chose "nothings" to nullify "somethings," "nobodies" to nullify "somebodies," so how can we ascribe glory to those we perceive to be powerful, whether because of their wealth or their wisdom? Paul's language of the "have-nots"—those who have nothing—in 1 Cor. 11 seems to echo this.

At the same time, Paul's apparently deliberate echo of Isa. 53 in his recounting of the Last Supper reminds participants of something vital: they are there at the table only because of someone else's sacrifice. The tradition of Eucharist can only be "handed over" *to* them because someone else was "handed over" *for* them. They have done nothing to earn their place at the table or to warrant a particular place

of honor; were it not for the place-taking of another, their iniqui-
ties would still be stacked against them. They are at this table only
because Jesus deserves to be there and they are united to him. The
Lord's Supper declares that their identity is a graced one and demands
that this grace be brought to bear in their evaluation of others.

Taken together, these strands of meaning from the Lord's Supper
ought to have a profound impact on our moral identity: by grace I
have been united to Jesus and therefore share in his holiness, as do
others who profess that he is Lord. I cannot boast; I cannot claim any
moral or intellectual capital that deserves to be respected by others; I
can only give thanks or, to use the Greek term for this, "eucharist." As
I reach out with the gospel to the world, I do it as someone who has
no reason to boast; as I seek to train and to teach others about God, I
do it as someone who has no reason to boast; and as I relate to other
parts of the church, I do it as someone who has no reason to boast.

But here is where the rubber might start to melt on the road. What
if my purity doesn't extend into my private life? What if it extends
only to the public realm where people see my "righteousness"? What
if my church shows me a degree of respect that exceeds that shown
to someone else because I apparently know more than they do about
the Bible or about doctrine? What if I show deference and respect to
a smart, well-dressed fellow academic or pastor that I don't show to
someone who is unemployed or who has mental health problems?
If an eminent Bible teacher were to turn up at your church on Sun-
day, would you clamor to meet him, and would you want to speak
to him more than you would want to speak to the old widow who
always demands a hug from you? If so, and ask this very slowly and
carefully, why?

For Paul, this is because we are still encased in bodies that are
constitutionally compromised by sin. The resurrection of Jesus bears
upon our lives, but our bodies still feel heavy with corruption and
chained to their graves. They still instinctively reach for idols. Our
next chapter will look in more depth at the way our new identity and
our old one relate. But Paul's response to the persistence of "the flesh"
is at key points to take us to the sacraments and their declaration of
identity. That declaration involves memory: we remember a particular
moment in time, a particular point in the story of the world that is

now *our* story. That memory is not ours but someone else's, and yet we play it over and over again because it tells us who we are. We are covenant members, beneficiaries of an act of place-taking that does more than simply excuse us: it defines us.

Conclusion

This chapter has considered the way Paul draws on a tradition of performed memory associated with the Passover to represent and foster Christian moral identity *in Christ*. We eat a meal, as Jesus and his disciples ate a meal, which is invested with memories that define identities. They are memories not of things that happened to us but of things that happened to someone else. Yet by performing them, we make them our own. We inhabit them, and they shape our sense of who we are.

For Paul, this does more than simply evoke a sense that we are defined by our relationship with Jesus. It shapes the way we think about that definition and its implications for how we live. This is one of the key points at which my own account of moral identity and transformation differs from those often labeled as belonging to the "apocalyptic Paul" school; my account moves closer to a Calvinist rather than a Lutheran interpretation of Paul. I take this position because Paul retains many of the covenantal allusions that mark the Passover and brings in some of the categories of the covenant. In particular, he brings covenantal purity to bear on ethical questions that range from participation in civic idol feasts to sexual immorality. His thinking is shaped deeply by the covenant and by the law as it bears on ritual matters. While his thinking about the law in relation to the origin and character of his own righteousness may have changed, he has not abandoned its normative function in Christian ethics, where it helps to show what is good and what is bad. In fact, as Bradley Bitner has recently highlighted, the law plays a key role in the distinctive constitution of the Corinthian church, setting it apart from the city of Corinth in general by having its own moral and economic distinctiveness.[9] Broadly, this recognition is reflected in the

9. Bitner, *Paul's Political Strategy in 1 Corinthians 1–4.*

Reformed traditions influenced by Calvin, which tend to operate with a covenant theology that continues to appreciate the value of the law.

In relation to discipleship, the obvious point is that our own practices should reflect this emphasis on the sacrament. The Eucharist or Lord's Supper should play a crucial role in our efforts to form Christians as disciples. Rather than being the empty routine that it sometimes is for us, or the individualistic enactment of receiving Christ, it should be undertaken consciously as an act of performative memory, done in the presence of God's Spirit, by which we define ourselves in union with Christ. By inhabiting *that* particular memory, we define ourselves over against worldly values, take up the cross, and align ourselves with God. And we do so together, as a diverse multitude united to the one God through the one mediator by the one Spirit, with a unity represented in the one loaf we eat and the one cup we drink. That is, we define ourselves in contrast to the world but in solidarity with one another. We have come out of Egypt in Christ our Passover and have done so together. If we live in a way that fails to discern the unity of Christ's body and subdivides it on the basis of doctrine or perceived worth, we eat and drink judgment on ourselves. That hardly squares with the idea that our response to the gospel is immaterial.

Up to this point I have said little about the way the Lord's Supper orients us toward the future: we proclaim his death "until he comes" (1 Cor. 11:26). The locatedness of the Christian life between the advent and return of Jesus, and the implications of this for our identity, will be the substance of our next two chapters, but at this point we can make a simple observation. Like baptism, the Lord's Supper dramatically performs the past of Jesus in a way that directs us toward his future and affirms that this future will be ours as well. The Lord's Supper reminds us, every time we participate in it, that our current moral condition is not our final state. More important, it reminds us that the final state will not be reached through a gradual process of moral growth but will involve a further, disjunctional event that will change everything decisively. He will come, and we will be changed.

5

Crying "Abba" in the Ruins of War

The Spirit and the Presence of Christ

In the last chapter, we considered the representation of Christian identity that is rendered in the Lord's Supper and closed by noting that while we remember the past of Jesus, we anticipate his future: we proclaim his death "until he comes." We are, then, identified between two points—in what is sometimes labeled "the tension of the already and the not yet"—and the space that we occupy is one marked by conflict. There are various ways that this conflict is represented and related to the experience of the Christian life, and the purpose of this chapter is to consider these. Much of this will, I am sure, be fairly familiar to the reader. Considering the texts in relation to moral identity, though, may cause us to appreciate some familiar issues in somewhat different ways: the tension we experience is not just about what we do and the context in which we do it but about who we are now and who we will be.

The title of this chapter is intended to evoke two texts in particular within the Pauline corpus, Rom. 8:15 and Gal. 4:6, though we will explore a little more broadly around Paul's writings. These texts continue to develop the sense that our identity is located "between times," involving a dramatic war between the old and the new, the flesh and the spirit, that will leave us crying in anguish to God. Crucial to these texts and to Paul's moral thought more widely is a recognition that this conflict involves the pitting of "sonly" identity against sin. While we may desire to use more inclusive gender language to describe the Christian life, this particular term is vital because it represents our conflict with sin and flesh as a manifestation of the particular moral identity of Jesus the Son working in us. This recognition is critically important for how we speak of and understand the place of the Spirit in the conflicts of the Christian life: if we don't properly comprehend the sonly character of the Christian life, we will tend to see the Spirit simply as an infused power that gives us the strength to do what we could not do without him, a supplement that will give us energy to keep going beyond our normal limits. If we do appreciate the sonly character of the conflict, though, we will recognize the importance of Paul's identification of the Spirit as "the Spirit of his Son" (Gal. 4:6). This will have an enormous impact on how we conceive of the Spirit and his work in us.

Galatians 4: Adoption and Christian Identity

In the first two chapters of this book, we traced some of the key lines of thought through Paul's Epistle to the Galatians. We saw that his autobiographical account builds toward the statement "It is no longer I who live, but Christ who lives in me" (Gal. 2:20) and that his core description of Christian identity in 3:26–27 centers on the significance of baptism: as many as have been "baptized into Christ" have clothed themselves with him.

In Gal. 4:1–7, he unpacks what this means for us: we have put on Christ the Son and as a result share in his relational cry of "Abba, Father."

> I mean that the heir, as long as he is a child, is no different from a slave, though he is the owner of everything, but he is under guardians and managers until the date set by his father. In the same way we also, when we were children, were enslaved to the elementary principles of the world. But when the fullness of time had come, God sent forth his Son, born of woman, born under the law, to redeem those who were

under the law, *so that we might receive adoption as sons*. And because you are sons, God has sent *the Spirit of his Son* into our hearts, crying, "Abba! Father!" So you are no longer a slave, but a son, and if a son, then an heir through God. (emphasis added)

What is emphasized particularly in this text is that the purpose of God's work of salvation is "so that" (*hina*) we might receive "adoption as sons" (4:5). The word for adoption is *huiothesia*, and it is a word often seen as having a Roman legal background. As I have highlighted elsewhere, it is a word that is distinctly applied to believers and to the new relationship with God into which they are brought; it is never applied to Jesus.[1] He is the Son not because of an act of adoption but because of his own ontological relationship to the Father. He is distinctly and uniquely "the Son," and this determines the significance of his sending by the Father. We are the ones who are adopted.

1. Some have argued that Rom. 1:3–4 ("concerning his Son, who was descended from David according to the flesh and was declared [or "appointed"] to be the Son of God in power according to the Spirit of holiness by his resurrection from the dead, Jesus Christ our Lord") should be read as indicating the adoption of Jesus to the special status of "the Son." This is understood to reflect the earliest Christology, traceable also in the Gospels, which considers Jesus to be a normal human who is specially empowered with the Spirit as he is adopted into the messianic role. Much turns on the significance of the word *horisthentos*, which can be rendered as "appointed," "determined," or (as in most translations) "declared," but the use of the word "flesh" is also important. While classic Christology understands the passage in terms of Christ's two natures, those advocating the adoptionist position argue that the references to flesh and Spirit should be read with the eschatological force that they often carry in Paul. That is, "flesh" is associated with the old, powerless, natural condition, while the "Spirit" is associated with the new, potent, liberated reality of the kingdom. Romans 1:3–4, then, describes Jesus from the point of view of the old condition (1:3) and the new (1:4). Within the latter, he is adopted to the position of Son of God. The view is particularly associated with James Dunn and developed in a number of his technical articles, notably "Jesus—Flesh and Spirit." It is also reflected in his classic study *Christology in the Making*, 33–36. Against this, it should be noted that Paul does not use the technical vocabulary of adoption with respect to Jesus (*huiothesia* etc.). His status as Son appears instead to be a given. Further, the case is problematized by the evidence that Paul considered the Son to be preexistent with God through eternity and to have taken the form of a servant (e.g., Phil. 2:6–8) as an act of descent. Methodologically, Paul's apparently standard identification of Jesus as God should drive the interpretation of Rom. 1:3–4, rather than that particular text driving our evaluation of his Christology more broadly. For the case that Paul's earliest Christology is, in fact, as high as one can imagine, see Bauckham, *God Crucified*.

Because of its legal background, "adoption" is principally a category of status. It does not necessarily indicate any love or warmth or reciprocity between parties but merely identifies the distinctive status enjoyed by those who have been adopted. Whereas before they were without name and identity, now they bear the name of the father and are treated as his heirs. But Paul doesn't leave adoption as a mere legal category. Because we are sons, God has sent the Spirit of *his* Son into our hearts. That Spirit causes the reciprocal relationship between the Father and the Son to be reprised within us: by him we cry, "Abba, Father." That cry is meaningful and powerful because it is Christ's cry, yet it truly comes from our lips; it is *we* who cry it. We do not do something that merely resembles or imitates Christ's sonly interaction with the Father; what we do participates in that interaction. Our cry of Abba is not *like* his cry; it *is* his cry, because we utter it by *his* Spirit.

So adoption becomes more than just a legal category of status, though it retains this force. Adoption becomes a richer category for the nature of our new covenant friendship with God; it describes our relationship in terms of participation in the sonly relationship of Jesus to the Father. The Spirit makes that participation a real thing: we really are sons who address God with all the intimacy of the eternal Son, because he is the Spirit of the Son. The Spirit is not an autonomous presence in our life; he is the one by whom the Son is present.

As an aside, this is another reason why social trinitarianism can be so problematic for our accounts of the Christian life. If we emphasize the threeness of God without properly prioritizing the oneness, as that oneness is reflected in the Shema, then we can treat the Spirit as if he were a person in his own right, conceivable apart from the other persons of the Trinity and conceptualized according to modern notions of personhood. This is true of each of the persons of the Trinity, but with the Spirit there is a particular problem related to sanctification: we can think of him as leading us toward the fulfillment of our selves through his particular agency and lose sight of the inalienably christomorphic character of Christian sanctification. The Spirit realizes and fulfills the identity of Christ in us. It is Christ's alien goodness that becomes ours.

This lies behind Paul's rejection of legalism in the following verses. The problem is not simply that seeking to obtain righteousness by performing the law is an impossible task and doomed to failure. Nor is it merely a "somewhat wrong" way of thinking about Christian morality. As we saw in the introduction, these are ways that we often think about legalism, but they fall short of truly identifying the problem. Legalism entails a return to the emptiness of the life that was not filled with the goodness of Jesus himself, effectively a return to an unbaptized life. This is the reason for Paul's earlier query—"Having begun with the Spirit, are you now trying to finish with the flesh?" (Gal. 3:3, my trans.)—and his emphasis on the place of the Spirit in God's overall purpose, reflected in his repeated use of the expression "so that" in the following quote:

> Christ redeemed us from the curse of the law by becoming a curse for us—for it is written, "Cursed is everyone who is hanged on a tree"—*so that* in Christ Jesus the blessing of Abraham might come to the Gentiles, *so that* we might receive the promised Spirit through faith. (Gal. 3:13–14, emphasis added)

These verses can now be seen as complementary to 5:4, where Paul indicates that those who are seeking to "be justified by the law" have cut themselves off from Christ. Precisely because the Spirit is his, and because the Spirit's role involves realizing Christ's moral presence in us, the abandonment of the Spirit is the abandonment of Christ. These are not two different things.

This representation of the Spirit as "the Spirit of Christ" is pivotal also to the right understanding of the conflict between flesh and spirit described later in Gal. 5:

> But I say, walk by the Spirit, and you will not gratify the desires of the flesh. For the desires of the flesh are against the Spirit, and the desires of the Spirit are against the flesh, for these are opposed to each other, to keep you from doing the things you want to do. But if you are led by the Spirit, you are not under the law. Now the works of the flesh are evident: sexual immorality, impurity, sensuality, idolatry, sorcery, enmity, strife, jealousy, fits of anger, rivalries, dissensions, divisions, envy, drunkenness, orgies, and things like these. I warn you, as I warned you

before, that those who do such things will not inherit the kingdom of
God. But the fruit of the Spirit is love, joy, peace, patience, kindness,
goodness, faithfulness, gentleness, self-control; against such things
there is no law. And those who belong to Christ Jesus have crucified the
flesh with its passions and desires. If we live by the Spirit, let us also
keep in step with the Spirit. Let us not become conceited, provoking
one another, envying one another. (Gal. 5:16–26)

Framed by what we have noted so far, the conflict or opposition that
is described here between these two sources of appetite or desire
manifests the Son's personal opposition to the evil that has become
part of the human constitution. The Spirit, in other words, is not an
independent power who just happens to be on the same moral page
as the Son but is the Spirit of the Son working in us.

Before we go any further, we should consider an important in-
sight from John Owen, a seventeenth-century Puritan theologian,
whose Christology makes a significant contribution to our thinking
about the operation of the Spirit within Jesus's own life. According
to Owen, the flesh of the mediator, of the man called Jesus, was
united to the Son and enjoyed the full goodness of the divine life by
the Spirit. Owen's point is essentially that whenever God acts upon
created stuff, he does so by the Spirit. So as the Son exists in hypostatic
union with mortal flesh, the Spirit is always at work in that union.[2]
The flesh of Jesus is not nakedly deified by the Son but by the Son's
presence within the union that is realized through the Spirit. Hence,
Jesus's miracles are credited on occasion to the Spirit or the finger
of God, and it is by the Spirit that he is raised from the grave (Matt.
12:28; Luke 11:20; Rom. 8:11). As the Son of God works good in the
human flesh that he himself takes, then, it is an activity realized by
the Spirit, and as the neurophysiology of that flesh embodies the will
of the Son, an alignment of divine will and human will occurs that
is actualized by the Spirit.

This perspective allows us to see how Gal. 5 works in relation to
the incarnation itself. It is not, of course, that the incarnation is just
a prototypical version of the Christian life, as someone like James

2. For a discussion of this element in Owen's thought, see Spence, *Incarnation
and Inspiration*.

Dunn would claim,[3] where God is present in the Christian through the Spirit in the same way that he was present in Jesus. This is why I stressed earlier that Jesus is never represented as an adopted Son: he is *the* Son, and that uniqueness is imprinted on the thought of all NT writers. But there is still a correspondence between what happened in the incarnation and what happens in us as our corrupt patterns of thought are transformed by the Spirit, our appetites are realigned, and our decisions are sanctified. In both cases, weak flesh is brought into proper communion with God through the work of the Spirit of the Son. That's where the hope of Christian optimism lies: "If the Spirit of him who raised Jesus from the dead dwells in you, he who raised Christ Jesus from the dead will also give life to your mortal bodies through his Spirit who dwells in you" (Rom. 8:11).

For all the failures we may have, attested in both biblical texts and pastoral experience, this fundamental optimism is vital to Paul's moral thought. Christ lives in you by his Spirit, and his goodness is able to renew the dereliction of your will. That, in fact, causes Paul's words in Gal. 5:17 to have rather more force than is sometimes recognized. One way of reading the Greek of this verse, advocated by Gordon Fee among others,[4] is that the opposition of flesh and Spirit is presented not as the explanation for why we struggle to live morally outstanding lives ("This is why you don't do what you want to do," my trans.) but as the reason not to follow our natural desires: "The flesh wants what is contrary to the Spirit, so you can't just do what you want; . . . you must allow yourself to be led" (my trans.).

This takes us into the heart of the dynamic of Christian identity, for it requires us to call ourselves into question and to see our *selves* as enacting two very different identities: one is our old self, outside Christ, enslaved to its own desires as it is led by the flesh; the other is our new self, in Christ, filled with his goodness and desiring what he desires as it is led by the Spirit. All of these images work together to say that we are called to a kind of *self*-distrust that is at the heart of mortification: rather than being confident in "who we are" (as the

3. As in Dunn's *Jesus and the Spirit* and "Rediscovering the Spirit." See also the theological conversation with James Mackey in Dunn and Mackey, *New Testament Theology in Dialogue.*

4. Fee, *Paul, the Spirit, and the People of God*, chap. 11, "The Ongoing Warfare."

spirit of the age would urge us to be), we are to have no confidence in the flesh but instead to seek to gain Christ and be found in him.

There is a real danger that some of our pastoral strategies within evangelicalism lack this emphasis. We may be seeking to train Christians to be confident moral agents who choose good and not evil because they know God's commandments and how to apply them in each and every situation, but we have not taught Christians to distrust themselves properly, to recognize that their flesh will take those commandments and make them serve our self-exaltation against God. We have not taught believers that they will keep themselves from becoming Pharisees or idolaters only if they see their flesh for what it is because their perceptions have been transformed by the Spirit of the Son. This does not turn us into insecure, nervous people who live by fear. Quite the opposite, it frees us from fear by directing us to set our lives within the life that will genuinely give us the certainty of hope. It involves the true "freedom of self-forgetfulness."[5] But it also forces us to see that the ghost image of our old self continues to be visible in our flesh and that we allow it to control us beyond its rightful tenure if we do not deliberately seek to be led by the Spirit.

The tenses and the moods of Paul's language are again instructive and frame this dynamic in important ways. It is not that we are dealing with a dualistic reality in which one self vies with the other for supremacy within us and the outcome is uncertain. Paul indicates in Gal. 5:24 that those who belong to Christ *have crucified* their flesh with its passions and desires; the tense is aorist (*estaurōsan*), and there is a sense that this event is completed. Our activity of mortification, of putting sin to death in our lives and bodies, is defined by this one irreversible event that took place outside ourselves: sin is beaten; we are made new in Christ. The manifestation of this reality, though, involves our application of this truth to our bodies. Paul uses the subjunctive mood in the verses that follow: "If we live by the Spirit, *let us* also keep in step with the Spirit." This is something that we must do.

Where Paul goes next with this is interesting, for he now asks why those who have come to enjoy this sonly relationship with

5. I borrow this expression from Keller, *Freedom of Self-Forgetfulness.*

God—knowing him because he has known them—are turning back
to their enslavement to false gods, to idolatry.

> Formerly, when you did not know God, you were enslaved to those that
> by nature are not gods. But now that you have come to know God, or
> rather to be known by God, how can you turn back again to the weak
> and worthless elementary principles [*stoicheia*] of the world, whose
> slaves you want to be once more? (Gal. 4:8–9)

We discussed the term *stoicheia* in chapter 3, noting that Paul seems
to associate it with a kind of constitutional idolatry at work as much
in the legalism of the Galatian group as in the syncretism of the
Colossian one. As we saw in that discussion, the root meaning of
the term labels members of a series, a usage that underlies its association with the elements of which the world is composed. To be
controlled by the *stoicheia*, the elements, is to be ruled by the world
and its dynamics. Interestingly, when Paul later directs his readers
to "keep in step with the Spirit" (Gal. 5:25), he actually uses the
cognate verb: *stoicheō*. Effectively, his message is that our lives have
been ordered by the basic schema of the world and our flesh by its
elements, its *stoicheia*, but now they are to be ordered by the Spirit.
We are to follow the *series* or the scheme of the Spirit. This will never
be easy, because our flesh and our thoughts will always want to be
aligned according to the series of the world; but to live according to
the grain of God's universe requires us to resist our natural instincts
and seek to be led by the Spirit. The manifestation of righteousness
in our lives may be passive; it may be the result of an agency outside
of ourselves, but it is not one in which we are inert.

Romans 6–7: "He Breaks the Power of Cancelled Sin"[6]

In Romans, we have a much fuller account of what it is to live under
the leading of the Spirit of the Son. According to traditional readings

---

6. This line is taken from Charles Wesley's classic hymn "O for a Thousand
Tongues to Sing" (1739). I quote it here because it captures a key element of the
gospel dynamic: sin has been canceled and its authority to condemn nullified, but
its power must still be broken in our lives.

of the book, the logic that unfolds through the opening chapters of
the letter is one that exposes the emptiness of seeking to accrue righteousness through our own activity, reaching its climactic statement,
"None is righteous, no, not one. . . . All have turned aside" (Rom.
3:10, 12). That last statement, of course, invokes the language of Isa.
53, and there lies the hope: an act of place-taking will bring about
both the righteousness that could not be accomplished by weak flesh
and the transformation that could not occur for those under sin's
curse. As a result of that act, there is now no condemnation for those
who are in Christ, but even more so, there is now hope that their lives
will be filled with the goodness of Christ himself. We died with him,
and we will also live with him; this hope is not simply for life beyond
the grave but for a life that is marked by Christ's own moral identity.
This is the logic that leads us to Rom. 6 and its profound demands
that we refuse sin's attempt to rule us:

> Let not sin therefore reign in your mortal body, to make you obey its
> passions. Do not present your members to sin as instruments for un-
> righteousness, but present yourselves to God as those who have been
> brought from death to life, and your members to God as instruments
> for righteousness. For sin will have no dominion over you, since you
> are not under law but under grace. (Rom. 6:12–14)

Notice that sin is personified in Paul's language: it is not just a
thing we do but a power that rules and controls. It is the big thing
composed of those beggarly elements of the world, the *stoicheia*. I
have often wondered whether Paul's thinking about sin as a personal
force is shaped by the language we encounter in the story of Cain
and Abel, where sin is described using language befitting a wilderness demon: it is "crouching at the door," desiring to rule (Gen.
4:7). Sin is not something that serves our free will; it is something
that seeks to exercise dominion over it. But its authority has now
been overthrown, and we cannot permit it to reign freely in our
lives again.

So far, so optimistic. But when we move into Rom. 7, it feels like we
have gone back to talking about someone who has not been delivered
from sin. We read of someone who says the following:

> For we know that the law is spiritual, but I am of the flesh, sold under sin. For I do not understand my own actions. For I do not do what I want, but I do the very thing I hate. Now if I do what I do not want, I agree with the law, that it is good. So now it is no longer I who do it, but sin that dwells within me. For I know that nothing good dwells in me, that is, in my flesh. For I have the desire to do what is right, but not the ability to carry it out. For I do not do the good I want, but the evil I do not want is what I keep on doing. Now if I do what I do not want, it is no longer I who do it, but sin that dwells within me. (Rom. 7:14–20)

All of us, I suspect, know precisely the kind of helplessness and shame this passage expresses: pastorally, it describes what we frequently experience as Christians. But since it sounds so much at odds with what was said in Rom. 6, many have argued that this is actually a memory of life apart from Christ, of Paul's pre-Christian self as he struggled with sin unaided. Scholars will often point to some of the finer details of verb tenses and pronouns to justify their position, and it is a view that is not without warrant in the text.[7]

However, the text can also be read as making good sense of our Christian failures, even as it describes a life apart from Christ. The key lies precisely in the way it considers moral identity. Remember what we have seen up to this point: the Christian self is one in which "I no longer live, but Christ lives in me," and the process of sanctification is represented as putting off the old, self-enclosed me that has now died and putting on the new me-in-Christ that lives through the Spirit of the Son. Our baptism is linked to this putting off and putting on of old and new identities, but the identities themselves exist between the already and the not yet. When we look back at Rom. 7, what do we notice? Most obviously, it is dominated by that first-person pronoun, "I." It is widely recognized that the early chapters of Romans are characterized by the third-person plural language of "they," "their," and "them," as in Rom. 1:21: "For although they knew God, they did not honor him as God or give thanks to him, but they became futile in their thinking, and their foolish hearts were

---

7. Open any commentary on Romans, and the issues will quickly emerge. An excellent though dense discussion of the passage is found in Ridderbos, *Paul*, 126–30.

darkened." This negative evaluation of "them" runs through 1:18–32. It then gives way to a passage in second-person singulars addressed to "you, O man [*anthrōpe*]," which runs throughout Rom. 2. Through the course of Rom. 3, Paul shifts to using first-person plurals, "we," to emphasize that he and other Jews share the plight of sin with everyone else: "All have sinned and fall short of the glory of God" (Rom. 3:23). When he goes on to speak of salvation in Christ, in the following chapters, these first-person plurals continue to dominate his language.

But when we reach Rom. 7:7, this pattern changes, and Paul shifts to using the first-person singular, "I."[8] The shift is dramatic and accompanies a turn toward speaking of the author's powerlessness to deal with sin and the complexity of his relationship to the law. All of this sends a strong set of cues to the reader that what we are reading about here is not the joyful condition of deliverance that "we" enjoy in Christ but the wretched condition that "I" inhabit apart from Christ. Those who consider the passage to speak of the pre-Christian self are, I think, correct: this is the old self talking, the old self failing to restrain sin and to attain righteousness. It is what Ridderbos labels the "I-myself" self, whose track record in dealing with sin is so lamentable.

But this does not mean that the words do not describe Christian experience, for the process of sanctification is one in which the old self's way of thinking and acting always seeks to reestablish itself and always needs to be denied or "put off" (cf. Eph. 4:22; Col. 3:9), something we do not always do successfully. And this persistence of the old self's way of thinking can occur within those who genuinely love God; it is not simply a feature of those who have backslidden in some dramatic way. Beverly Gaventa highlights that the language of Rom. 7, particularly concerning the author's delight in the law and its goodness (7:22), evokes the language of the Psalter, especially psalms such as 119, which express deep love for God's commandments. By evoking the voice of the psalmist who says, "How I love your law!" (Ps. 119:97), and then identifying the one who so speaks as helpless to actually obey that law, Paul communicates something of the conflicts

---

8. For an excellent discussion of these shifts, see Gaventa, "Shape of the 'I.'"

and failures that mark us daily. Even those who truly love God and his word will be helpless to resist sin unless they are delivered.

But the answer is not the newer and more stringent moral discipline that we often commit ourselves to, saying, "This time I will be more rigorous about prayer and reading, and I won't fall as easily next time temptation comes along." This is precisely what we often do in response to our failures, and it is often what we formalize in our programs of discipleship. It plays on the particular vulnerability that emerges from sin's inward turn: having curved in on ourselves in sin, we seek the solution to our plight in an inwardly curved way, as something found in our selves if we will only discipline those selves more carefully. At that point, we say not "I no longer live, but Christ lives in me" but "I live (but badly), and I must do this (to be better)." That way has not worked yet and never will. What we do will be abominable, and for those who have come to love Jesus, the abomination will be seen for what it is. We will cry out, "Wretched man that I am! Who will deliver me from this body of death?" (Rom. 7:24).

The process of mortifying the old self continues to devolve upon us as a Christian responsibility, and it is not an easy one; it is a serious business. When Paul indicates that the way to life is for us to "put to death the deeds of the body" by the Spirit (Rom. 8:13), he presents the Christian life as something that does indeed involve forceful effort. That effort includes the discipline of closing down our plans for sin before they turn into action: we are to "make no provision for the flesh, to gratify its desires" (the second part of Rom. 13:14). But Paul's representation of this tough activity of mortification and self-discipline centers on the personal image that we saw to be at work in his account of baptism: we are deliberately to "put on the Lord Jesus Christ" (the first part of Rom. 13:14). When Paul speaks of us putting on our new self in Eph. 4:24, it is literally "the new man" (*anthrōpos*) that we are to don, an expression that draws upon his previous use of the language of "new man" in 2:15. It is an expression that points not to an upgraded or remodeled version of myself but to Jesus and my participation in *him*. Hence, when the one who has sinned cries, "Wretched man that I am! Who will deliver me from this body of death?" (Rom. 7:24), the only answer that will truly bring hope is the one that Paul articulates with a proclamation of gratitude: "Thanks be to God through Jesus Christ our Lord!" (Rom. 7:25). It is an answer shaped by the recognition that we need a deliverer to rescue us, not just from guilt but from sin's crouching power itself. The thanksgiving here is not just for forgiveness but for liberation; it is crucial that we allow it to inform the way that we think about Christian discipline and rigor—mortification—so that they are thoroughly Christ-centered.

One important point that despite its obviousness is often overlooked is that the expression of thanks makes no reference to the Holy Spirit. We might expect it to, given the way that we often think about the Christian life. Our particular theology may consider deliverance from the body of death to come through the Spirit, as if he were the solution to our enslavement, the one who will rescue us from this body of death. But at this point, only God and Jesus are mentioned. As we shall see in our next chapter, the Spirit's ministry is described in some depth in Rom. 8, so it is not that Paul minimizes or marginalizes his significance. But the Spirit is not, in himself, the one who delivers us from the body of death: Jesus is. The Spirit *realizes* the deliverance that is accomplished by and in Jesus. This is important for the proper conception of that deliverance: it is always a matter of participation in Christ, and the description of the Spirit's ministry in Rom. 8 will reflect this.

The complexity of Christian experience as something lived "between the times" is further attested by the rest of 7:25: "Thanks be to God through Jesus Christ our Lord! So then, I myself serve the law of God with my mind, but with my flesh I serve the law of sin." Again, these words will resonate with each of us; the need to put off our old self continues to devolve upon us, for its habits are deeply ingrained. Only by continually experiencing the radically free presence of our deliverer can we see those patterns altered, and along the way we will experience much personal failure. The pastoral significance of the words with which Rom. 8 begins is striking: "There is therefore now no condemnation for those who are in Christ Jesus." All of the themes that have been swirling around up to this point resurface throughout the next few verses: what the law, because of the weakness of flesh, was powerless to do (i.e., to actually deliver us from sin), God has done by sending his Son in our likeness so that the just requirement (*dikaiōma*) of the law might be fulfilled in us who walk by the Spirit (8:2–4).

In the next chapter, we will trace where Rom. 8 goes from here. We will consider the actual experience of the Spirit's work and the reality of the transformation that goes with it, as the Christian cries, "Abba! Father!" This is not in the context of a perfected freedom but in the ruins of a war still going on in and around us. The key, as we will see, is prayer. For now, we can appreciate the forceful honesty of Paul in his representation of the gospel. Having led his readers from a bleak evaluation of the human moral condition—"None is righteous, no, not one" (Rom. 3:10)—to the peace with God that has come through the gospel (5:1) and to the hope that sin's reign is at an end, Paul returns to speak of the reality of sin as a pervasive and manipulative force. Sin continues to squat in our minds after its tenure has been ended. It always seeks to turn us in on ourselves. Even in our efforts to resist it, we can end up serving it, because those efforts are so often defined by what "I" will do to discipline myself. The only thing that will break this cycle of self-centeredness is asking the right question: not "What can I do?" but "Who can deliver me?" The same Jesus by whom sin's debt is canceled is the one by whom its power is broken.

Conclusion

This chapter has focused on the manifestation of Christian moral identity here and now in our lives. That temporal detail is important, because *here and now* we do not live in a world from which sin has been finally vanquished. Our identity in Christ is always assaulted and continues to be at odds with what the bodies that we occupy have always done, habitually and naturally. One day our bodies will be transformed, and we will no longer inhabit such weak flesh. But until then, we must intentionally put off the instinctive habits and reactions of our old self, which are now wired into our neurology,[9]

---

9. Research into addiction has long recognized that our habits are linked to the patterns of connections in our brain and particularly in what is known as "the reward center." Once we do something and enjoy it, it becomes more natural and instinctive to do it again because the pattern begins to be established. The recognition of the role that the reward center plays has been an important part of the shift from seeing

and put on the deliberative goodness of the new man. The gendered quality of this new self is unavoidable because it is very specifically the identity of the man Jesus, the Son of God. Our donning of *his* identity, our union with *his* self, involves adoption: we become "sons," whether or not we are male by nature, because our relationship with the Father is a participation in *his* relationship with him. Wonderfully, that means it is secure and beyond question.

Our new moral life, then, is a matter not of becoming better versions of ourselves, whatever gender we might be, but of participating in him. It is *sonly* identity, and this is what the Spirit works to realize within us. We will return to this gendered dimension in our final chapter because it has some implications for how we think about the continuation of our own personal particularities in union with Christ. God's "sons" are not confined to the male gender, and this will be an interesting point to consider. At the same time, we cannot and must not lose the gendered specificity of the word "sons," because it is tied to the personal uniqueness of the one in whom we are saved, *the* Son.

Paul is savagely honest about the manifestation of our new identity in Christ. It will come with struggle because we live in a sinful world, in bodies that still remember their old identities and their old habits. Sin may have been dethroned, but it will still pretend to own us. As we saw from Rom. 7, our return to sin and our experience of feeling that we are still its slaves are really manifestations of our old selves, which were separated from Christ. Even our shame-filled reactions to our sins can be Christless and self-centered if we seek to deal with the problem of our sin without asking that key question: "Who will deliver me from this body of death?"

When we answer that question rightly by naming Jesus Christ, there is hope and joy. We echo Paul's statement "Thanks be to God

---

addiction only in chemical or physiological terms (i.e., in relation to substance addiction) to seeing it as a complex neurophysiological problem that can involve behaviors as much as substances. Such studies have also revealed that one of the key problems in addiction is a tendency to see one's identity and "wiring" as fixed, where in truth they continue to be highly plastic. Neural patterns of addiction can be rewired by our behavior, just as new patterns of addiction can be generated by our behavior. It is interesting that a key element in the positive rewiring of the addicted brain is generally understood to involve a breaking down of an addict's sense of self-identity and self-importance.

through Jesus Christ our Lord!" (Rom. 7:25). We find relief and rest in the knowledge that there is "now no condemnation for those who are in Christ Jesus" (8:1). We are still in the ruins of war, and when we address God our Father, it is often not with a triumphant shout but with a pained cry of "Abba, Father." But the war is won, and the signs of that victory will be manifest in us with a beauty and reality that is not refuted by our failures. In the next chapter, we will consider this in relation to Rom. 8.

6

One Little Victory

Hope and the Moral Life

Several times already in this book we have thought about the way
Christian moral identity looks back to the past of Jesus while
also looking forward to his future. By linking Jesus's past and
future to Christian moral identity and understanding that identity
as constituted by the acting presence of Christ in our lives now, we
see it in terms very different from the ones in which it is often cast.
We do not only look back at a past event from which we benefit, a
transaction made on our behalf, and we do not only look forward
to a future in which we will be definitively better. We look back to a
past that is ours now, and as with all backstories, it defines who we
are. At the same time, we look forward to a future that will bring
to its perfect realization what we genuinely are, as we are in Christ.
In one sense, the perfection we will enjoy is scarcely imaginable, for
we will see clearly what we now behold only in a mirror. In another
sense, we know what it will look like because we know Jesus, and
our anticipation is shaped by our retrospection. It is vital, then, that
we hold the retrospective and the prospective together—both focused on the mediator, Jesus—and allow them to shape the Christian
moral life as one that *really* involves an experience of the goodness of

God manifest in us, while affirming that this is, as yet, an imperfect experience.

Those familiar with certain strands in modern theology, particularly some of the developments of Barthian theology that have had a deep effect on Pauline studies, will appreciate why this claim of a real and transforming experience of God's goodness is significant.[1] A misplaced emphasis on the perfection of divine grace and a dislocation of Christology from its classical contexts in both theology proper and the economy of salvation have led some to place little stock in the meaningful experience of growth in the Christian life. More traditional accounts of sanctification are often seen to lack a proper emphasis on grace because they retain a place for some kind of work undertaken by the believer.

This approach, though, is too neglectful of the Spirit's place in the writings of Paul: the Spirit realizes the victory of Christ within us. Each act of faith, each act of obedience, however small, is a participation in this reality; one little victory is, in truth, a manifestation of the presence of divine goodness in our lives, which is both affirmed and carried forward by our hope.

This chapter will consider these themes, particularly as they emerge from Rom. 8. We will think a little more about a concept that, to this point, we have said little about: conforming to the likeness of Christ. We will think also about the way prayer is represented as the core dynamic of this participation. And within the practice of prayer, we will think about the prominence of the themes of gratitude and patient supplication. But all will be considered in relation to what seems so evident in Rom. 8: our experience of goodness is always contextualized by badness, and our hope lies in the sure conviction that the badness will not outbid it in the end.

> You, however, are not in the flesh but in the Spirit, if in fact the Spirit of God dwells in you. Anyone who does not have the Spirit of Christ does not belong to him. But if Christ is in you, although the body is dead because of sin, the Spirit is life because of righteousness. If the Spirit of him who raised Jesus from the dead dwells in you, he who

1. See the discussion of Douglas Campbell and others in chap. 1, "Scholarly Contexts for the Present Study."

raised Christ Jesus from the dead will also give life to your mortal bodies through his Spirit who dwells in you. (Rom. 8:9–11)

The language that Paul uses in these verses and the correspondences that he establishes should now be unsurprising, for they reflect the patterns that we have traced through the course of this book. His assertion that his readers are not in the flesh but in the Spirit corresponds directly to his statement that Christ lives in them. Taken together, these two sides of the reality of their lives mean that they are no longer in the condition of essential hostility to God that Paul associates with the mind set on the flesh (8:7–8). There is a reality that has not gone away; they still have dead bodies, but they also have the living Spirit within them: "Although the body is dead because of sin, the Spirit is life because of righteousness" (Rom. 8:10). That combination sets the tone for what follows: the Spirit will give life to their dead bodies, an image that echoes Ezekiel's valley of dry bones. By the Spirit's enabling, ironically, Christians will mortify the deeds of their dead bodies, making them truly dead. By the Spirit, they will refuse to allow their native weakness to govern them.

In 8:15, Paul replicates the language that we have already seen him use in Gal. 4:6: "We have received the Spirit of adoption, by whom we cry, 'Abba, Father!'" (my trans.). Strikingly, the Spirit is defined here by his role in relation to adoption, which, as we have seen repeatedly, is the matter of our union with the Son. The cry here really does sound like it emerges from the anguish of our struggles. In the midst of all the anxieties and concerns that arise from living in a still sin-filled world, perhaps not least the crises of assurance that result from the kind of failure described in Rom. 7, the Spirit co-testifies with our spirit that we are sons (Rom. 8:16). The word used in Greek, symmartyreō, is one of numerous syn-prefixed words in Rom. 8, most of which are connected to our relationship with Christ. The prefix syn means "together with" and is attached to the verbs in a way that we might capture with hyphens in our English translations. The point here is that, by themselves and apart from the gospel, our spirits would have no such assurance. The spirits of those to whom Paul writes will naturally quail at the scale of evil that surrounds them and that fills them, but their spirits are co-identified with the Spirit of Christ, and they share in his testimony to their sonship. They cry, "Abba, Father," and no accusation can take away from the legitimacy of that address.

Interestingly, Paul then describes them as "children" (*tekna*), a term that takes us beyond the language of "sons" (*huioi*) used to this point, which might be taken as rather coldly pointing to a legal concept of adoption (*huiothesia*). Now, however, they are children coming into the presence of a Father. The shift in language suggests something more familial, more intimate, and something bolder: for all the shame believers may feel over their last worst sin, they rush to the arms of their Papa.[2]

But they come as those who are suffering, and it is to this that Paul speaks with his language of hope:

> For I consider that the sufferings of this present time are not worth comparing with the glory that is to be revealed to us. For the creation waits with eager longing for the revealing of the sons of God. For the creation was subjected to futility, not willingly, but because of him who subjected it, in hope that the creation itself will be set free from its bondage to corruption and obtain the freedom of the glory of the children of God. For we know that the whole creation has been groaning together in the pains of childbirth until now. And not only the creation, but we ourselves, who have the firstfruits of the Spirit, groan inwardly as we wait eagerly for adoption as sons, the redemption of our bodies. For in this hope we were saved. Now hope that is seen is not hope. For who hopes for what he sees? But if we hope for what we do not see, we wait for it with patience. (Rom. 8:18–25)

Notice that the whole of creation looks forward to adoption, *huiothesia*. This is what it is all about: the elect sharing in the sonship of Christ by the activity of his Spirit. Participation in his sonship is

2. James Barr ("'*Abbā* Isn't 'Daddy'") argues against the notion that "Abba" is simply equivalent to the English "Daddy," as popularized by Joachim Jeremias. Barr insists that the Aramaic word maintains a sense of respect for the father that is not characteristic of the English one and would be carried into adulthood as an address to a parent in a way that "Daddy" generally is not. Having said this, the word does have an important familial warmth to it. Tim Keller (*Prayer*, 299n143) captures this nicely: "When an adult continues to call a parent Mama or Papa, it mixes respect with the old intimacy, delight, and access that they had as little children."

the thing that the story of the Bible has been all about, but here that adoption is not a *fully* realized possession: it still awaits the redemption of our bodies. That is the hope for which we "wait . . . with patience" and endurance (8:25). Our bodies have not yet experienced the fulfillment of their redemption.

Paul moves from this description of realistic hope, this acknowledgment that the present state is not all there is, to a further description of the Spirit helping us "in our weakness" (Rom. 8:26). The language here is the language of intercession and prayer. The Spirit's intercession is represented as something that takes the communicative act of prayer that is compromised by our state of fleshly weakness ("We do not know what to pray for as we ought," 8:26) and makes it real and substantive before God. What is prayed remains, to us, something beyond articulation—groans that words cannot express—yet the prayer is meaningful to God because he knows the mind of the Spirit. But these prayers derive their significance from the fact that they are a participation in the sonship of the Son. Our cry is, specifically, "Abba, Father," and this is the address that always directs our prayers.

The Spirit's intercession is also represented as being "according to the will of God" (Rom. 8:27). We pray not entirely comprehending what we are asking, and those prayers are taken to God by the indwelling Spirit, precisely in alignment with God's will. Our prayers, then, become a manifestation of God's will, a participation in his providential activity, even when we ourselves do not comprehend what those prayers truly mean. This, I think, is part of the significance of the imagery within the flow of the text. Our reference to the Spirit's intercession according to the will of God leads—through the statement that the one who searches hearts knows the mind of the Spirit—to the famous (and notoriously complicated) verse that for those who love him, those called according to his purpose, God works all things together for good (Rom. 8:28). However we understand this verse, it seems to render something of the providential mystery that God works to bring his creatures to flourish and that their prayers are a participation in this acting will. The point, again, is that we are not inert victims of providence but are prayerful participants because of the reality of the Spirit. God graciously and lovingly involves us in his work, just as fathers often do with their children.

But once again this takes a christomorphic turn. The purpose of God is that we are conformed "to the image [*eikōn*] of his Son" (Rom. 8:29). In the context of Rom. 8—with all its talk of struggle and enmity, of nakedness, danger, and sword—being conformed to the image of a Savior whom we know to have been crucified is hardly a triumphalist image. It is not a message of unqualified comfort that everything will be fine. Instead, it takes the sufferings of this present time and understands them christologically. Elsewhere, Paul will make a similar point even more explicitly:

> Blessed be the God and Father of our Lord Jesus Christ, the Father of mercies and God of all comfort, who comforts us in all our affliction, so that we may be able to comfort those who are in any affliction, with the comfort with which we ourselves are comforted by God. For as we share abundantly in Christ's sufferings, so through Christ we share abundantly in comfort too. If we are afflicted, it is for your comfort and salvation; and if we are comforted, it is for your comfort, which you experience when you patiently endure the same sufferings that we suffer. Our hope for you is unshaken, for we know that as you share in our sufferings, you will also share in our comfort. (2 Cor. 1:3–7)

By now in our study we should be sensitized to the participatory significance of these verses. They are not simply saying that we suffer in a way that is similar to Christ or that our sufferings have a similar outcome. They are saying that our experience of suffering is a sharing in his; they are, very precisely, the sufferings of Christ, experienced in union with him. The sufferings are not "for the gospel"—in the sense that they are things befalling us as a consequence of the gospel—but are, in fact, part of the gospel. They are given meaning precisely because they are the sufferings of Christ's body, because he participates in them even as they participate in him.

If this sounds like a mere play on language, let me draw out some of its significance. We often think of "cruciformity"[3] in the Christian

---

3. This language of cruciformity is prominent in the work of Michael Gorman, who has developed one of the more well-rounded accounts of Pauline soteriology and ethics. See his *Cruciformity* and *Inhabiting the Cruciform God*.

life as a matter of consciously living in self-sacrifice, perhaps even as a kind of moral heroism. But if we have a theologically rounded account of the cross, then we understand cruciformity as the climax of the sufferings of the one who takes all of human cursedness and frailty to himself, the one whom Paul describes as bearing the likeness of sinful flesh. The death is not just about punishment for sin, though it certainly includes that, but is more fully the uniting of the absolute wretchedness of the human condition to the glory of the Son. And that wretchedness is being redeemed even at the moment of its greatest sense of abandonment. "My God, my God, why have you abandoned me?" (Mark 15:34 CSB) is more than just the cry of the one who bears our sin; it is also the cry of the one who has united the absolute lostness of Adam's race to himself. To share in this is often to experience cruciformity not as glad self-sacrifice but as bewildered suffering. Sometimes we resemble Christ most at the points when we cry, "Why have you forsaken me?" Cruciformity often looks and feels like defeat.

At such moments, our simple ability to continue to cry "Abba, Father," the witness of the Spirit that we are sons of God through faith, the groaning that we utter without comprehending its real significance—these are important victories, and they derive *their* victorious significance from the shape of the one little victory that gives them meaning: the dying Galilean peasant crying in Aramaic to a Father of whose presence, at this particular point, he has no assurance. I am reminded often of the words of the late songwriter Mark Heard: sometimes "our hopes fall round our feet like the dust of dead leaves, and we end up looking like what we believe."[4]

There is a point of deep pastoral significance here: when we seek to give comfort to those who are devoid of assurance in a time of real suffering, perhaps an experience of real malice and evil, our task is to draw their eyes to the character of the suffering from which theirs derives its meaning.

This shapes the practices of hope and gratitude that Paul here and elsewhere indicates are to characterize our prayers. They are not

4. "The Orphans of God," track 4 on Mark Heard, *Satellite Sky*, Ideola Music/ ASCAP, 1992; Fingerprint Records, 1992.

necessarily outpourings of our perception that all is well but things that must be asserted even when our hearts and our senses can find no warrant for them. Read again these words with this in mind, noting the language of groaning and of the nonvisibility of our hope:

> And not only the creation, but we ourselves, who have the firstfruits of the Spirit, groan inwardly as we wait eagerly for adoption as sons, the redemption of our bodies. For in this hope we were saved. Now hope that is seen is not hope. For who hopes for what he sees? But if we hope for what we do not see, we wait for it with patience. (Rom. 8:23–25)

"Waiting," here, is an act of assertion in the face of the nonvisibility of our hope. It is a deliberate act of self-restraint, quieting the instincts that pressure us to act in our way rather than God's and submitting to his will and trusting in the timeline of his purpose. In 8:25, the verb "we wait" is qualified by the expression "with patience." In fact, the word translated "patience" here (*hypomonē*) could also be translated "endurance." This is not the sweet patience of an angler but the resilient endurance of a resistance group, whose members refuse to capitulate to their oppressors because they trust in the certainty of liberation. They assert their hope and refuse to despair.

And crucially, of course, those assertions are made as a response to the resurrection. They take their warrant not from any perception in ourselves but from an acknowledgment of the victory that is revealed in the resurrection as the firstfruits of God's triumph and the outpouring of the Spirit as an effect of that victory. This is the point of Paul's language in Rom. 8:11: "If the Spirit of him who raised Jesus from the dead dwells in you, he who raised Christ Jesus from the dead will also give life to your mortal bodies through his Spirit who dwells in you." Our hope is founded on our retrospective, not on the shifting reality of our mood. It acknowledges that the possibilities for my life are not defined by my flesh, with its heavy fragility and evident mortality; they are defined by Jesus Christ and by the Spirit who raised him from death. Because I am in him, and he is in me, there is a hope that my current state will not be a final state, but there is also an affirmation that this state is a real if imperfect union. And it is this union that is spoken of in the closing verses of Rom. 8:

What then shall we say to these things? If God is for us, who can be against us? He who did not spare his own Son but gave him up for us all, how will he not also with him graciously give us all things? Who shall bring any charge against God's elect? It is God who justifies. Who is to condemn? Christ Jesus is the one who died—more than that, who was raised—who is at the right hand of God, who indeed is interceding for us. *Who shall separate us from the love of Christ?* Shall tribulation, or distress, or persecution, or famine, or nakedness, or danger, or sword? As it is written,

> "For *your* sake we are being killed all the day long;
> we are regarded as sheep to be slaughtered."
> (Rom. 8:31–36, emphasis added)

The language in verse 35 of not being separated is the language of a bond that cannot be broken. All that we do, we do in a union with Christ that cannot be undone by mere tribulation or death; its victory over the latter has already been demonstrated in the resurrection. If that worst of deaths could not break it, neither can any other. The confidence of believers facing death and slaughter is precisely that they do so "for your sake" (8:36), as a participation in the sufferings of Jesus, and that this same involvement will unite them to the resurrection.

Conclusion

Participation in the sonly identity of Jesus is no easy thing. To have one's identity not just patterned but actually *constituted* by a Savior who gave himself for us—as we proclaim in the Eucharist—is to participate in a gospel that is as far from a message of earthly health and prosperity as it is possible to be. In our union with him, we share in his sufferings, and just as his sufferings occluded all sensory and affective awareness of God's care—causing him to cry, "My God, why have you forsaken me?"—so ours will often leave us feeling bewildered and bereft. But we have the Spirit of the Son in us, and when our own spirits have nothing to give and no hope in themselves, his Spirit lifts us up and helps us to trust and testify that we are the children of God. When our own spirits are too horrified to find the words of faith, his Spirit intercedes with groans that words cannot express. What horrifies us may lie in the world around us, but it may also lie within us, in the persistent malevolence of the old self that we saw described in Rom. 7. If we were self-contained, we could not pray, for our sense of who we are would prevent us from daring to speak in the presence of God. But we are not self-contained. We are contained in Christ's self and inhabited by his Spirit and able to testify quite truly that we are the children of God. In the midst of our moral failure and in the midst of our suffering, we genuinely manifest the reality of our adoption. Each little victory means something because it is a real participation in God's providential work in Christ. It is not undone by our failures and will not be outlasted by our old selves.

Our experience of adoption as a meaningful and conscious reciprocation of God's work in our behalf involves prayer. In prayer, our fellowship with the triune God is realized, with each person of the Trinity involving himself with us in distinctive ways. Prayer is the practice in which the elements of our new identity in Christ are asserted against our old self. It is the place where our passive reception of Christ's righteousness expresses itself with active verbs.[5]

Prayer, indeed, is the practice that brings together all the threads of what we have considered in this book. In prayer our covenant friendship with God is expressed as we come into his presence to speak with him. In prayer we acknowledge the acts that we have performed and confess that our hope lies in someone else. In prayer we orient ourselves toward the one whose identity we hope to inhabit. Most important, in prayer the dual subjecthood of our new identity is embodied: we are the ones who pray, the acting subjects of the verbs of prayer, but our prayers are co-testimonies with the Spirit or intercessions by him.

Crucially, though, our prayers are never forms of possession. It is not that the Spirit occupies us like a demon, switching off the lights and taking control of the strings. The Spirit co-testifies with our spirit

5. J. Todd Billings (*Calvin, Participation, and the Gift*) makes this point in relation to Calvin's theology of prayer, defending the Reformer against accusations that his understanding of salvation left no room for meaningful reciprocity. Billings highlights that Calvin's understanding of prayer involves a reciprocal human response to divine grace as a meaningful act of participation.

and intercedes with our groanings. This, indeed, parallels the way Paul represents our relationship with Jesus throughout Rom. 8, using a host of verbs that are combined with the prefix *syn*: our realities and Christ's are not buffered from each other but are linked. Our sufferings are a participation in his past; our hope is a participation in his future.

7

Concluding Synthesis

Living in Union with Christ

In this final chapter, I want to draw the threads of our exegetical discussion together and address some of the conceptual and pastoral issues in a way that is, on one level, more abstract, because it takes place above the immediate detail of the texts. Yet, on another level, it is more concrete, because it articulates truths in a manner intelligible to our late modern context.

"It Is No Longer I Who Live, but Christ Who Lives in Me": What Does This Mean?

At the beginning of this book, I indicated that any responsible account of Christian moral identity must start and finish with Paul's words in Gal. 2:20: "It is no longer I who live, but Christ who lives in me." But what does this actually mean? Does it mean that our particular identities are entirely effaced and we simply become localized instantiations of Jesus? Is that what Paul meant when he said that in Christ "there is neither Jew nor Greek, there is neither slave nor free, there is no male and female" (Gal. 3:28)?

Such a reading of Paul would not do justice to some of the key features of his writing. First, he still writes as "Paul"; this is the identification with which his letters begin. He does not title his letters as if they were messages from Jesus. This is not as glib an observation as it may sound. There are plenty of examples of pseudepigraphy in the ancient world, with a writer adopting the identity of a well-known figure. One plausible theory advanced for this is that it reflected some sense that the personage was being channeled by the author.[1] Many ancient pseudepigraphical works are, in fact, of Jewish provenance, so this practice would have been available to Paul as an option had he understood his new identity in this way. Instead, his writing style continues to draw on his personal particularity, even if that particularity is now understood in different terms.

Second, Paul also writes to people and churches that retain their particularity. He names individuals, both male and female, and speaks of their particular contributions. Third, his account of "the body of Christ" very specifically focuses on the diverse particularity that characterizes the church and the obligations on each member to show proper care for the others. All of this indicates that Paul's language is not intended to suggest that we are simply absorbed into Christ's identity, with our own particularities being dissolved in the process.

Neither is Christ-in-us a matter of possession. As we saw in our discussion of Rom. 8, Paul's language instead suggests some kind of co-subjecthood, in which Christ's Spirit works with ours. His Spirit and ours, which co-testify to adoption, remain distinct, even if they are collectively united to Christ. Taken by itself, Paul's statement in Gal. 2:20 could be read in either of these ways—as absorption or possession—but read in the context of the rest of his writing, it must be understood differently.

Instead, I suggest that we understand Paul's account of Christian moral identity to involve the following key elements. First, Paul has a profound sense that he is no longer self-contained and that his hope lies in the other personal reality that now inhabits him. He has been "de-autonomized," and the disruption of his sense of self-subsistence

1. This thesis is carefully developed by Vicente Dobroruka, *Second Temple Pseudepigraphy*.

is crucial to his new identity.[2] On one level, this mirrors the way that we are all, in truth, constituted through our relationships with others, particularly those with whom we share intimacy. The Scottish novelist Iain Banks captures this nicely in reflecting on the relationship between two lovers:

> You don't belong to her and she doesn't belong to you, but you're both part of each other; if she got up and left now and walked away and you never saw each other again for the rest of your lives, and you lived an ordinary waking life for another fifty years, even so on your deathbed you would still know she was part of you.
>
> You have left your marks on each other, you have helped to shape one another; you have each given the other an accent on their life which they will never quite lose; no matter.[3]

But this general, relational quality to our personhood—even in the rarified form that it is experienced within marriage—is not, in the end, adequate as an account of what it means to be united to Christ. Jesus is not just *a* significant other but for Christians *the* significant other, and the nature of our relationship to him is not simply one of natural interaction but one that involves indwelling. We are in him, and he is in us.

This way of thinking about our identity in Christ makes good sense of the importance of prayer to Paul's thought, especially in Rom. 8. Prayer is a way of relating; it is not something that can ever be done by a self-contained person who exists in isolation, but it always requires an "other" with whom we relate. In prayer we recognize that our personal concerns are not the horizons of our existence, that we do not exist of and for ourselves. We pray in communion with the Spirit, in communion with the Son, and both communions define our communion with the Father. No other relationship corresponds to this particular communion. Ordinary relationships might affect us profoundly, might give us thick accents, but only this communion can allow us to address God as "Abba." In prayer we live out our new, relationally constituted identity.

2. This is a key element in J. Louis Martyn's criticism of Engberg-Pedersen. See his essay "De-apocalypticizing Paul."
3. Banks, *The Bridge*, 378.

Second, Paul's sense of *who he is becoming*—his future self—is determined not by who he is in himself but by Jesus. It is not that he will become a better version of Paul, as in virtue theory, but he will come to inhabit the perfections of Jesus. When the Spirit works in him, it is not to improve Paul's better qualities and to eradicate the bad ones, so that Paul will eventually become as good as he could ever be. Rather, the Spirit works to unite Paul to the goodness of Jesus, so that *this* goodness manifests itself in the particularity of the apostle's life. The difference may seem to be subtle, but it actually constitutes an absolute distinction between two ways of thinking about the Christian's moral identity.

Third, and as a function of the first two points, Paul considers the potency of his new identity to flow entirely from the presence of Jesus and not from any strengths within his natural self. The natural Paul is entirely impotent to do good, but he is united to one whose potency is irrefutable. In union with him, Paul can do all things.

What does this look like for us? At the most basic level, it involves a recognition that we no longer define our own limits, because we no longer identify ourselves principally with the story that we have lived through our lives. I am helpless to break the cycles of sin in my life—I have seen that over and over again—and my limbs and neurons lack the potency to live a new story, but I am now united to Jesus Christ, identified principally by his story. I have performed this new identification in baptism and in Eucharist, allowing my own history to be redefined by his future as well as my own. I am aware that his Spirit indwells my limbs with all the vital goodness of Jesus himself. And so, when I face my everyday temptations, it is no longer inevitable that my story of failure will play itself out yet again. It is his story of victory that I expect to be reiterated in me. Today, tonight, tomorrow—the pattern that has always replayed in me (or in you) will be disrupted, because there is a new player involved.

Researchers into addiction have increasingly recognized the importance of "plasticity." Patterns of behavior that appear to be hardwired into our brains control us because we see no prospect that they can ever be changed. Recognizing that our brains are plastic, and hence can be retrained in such a way that destructive patterns do not have to repeat themselves, can be a crucial step in recovery. For the Christian, this plasticity is associated with the acting presence of Jesus through his Spirit. Failure is not inevitable, because we are indwelled by him.

As soon as I lose this focus and begin to see the moral challenge as one that I face myself, drawing on my own resources, I have failed. I may look victorious, and I may take credit for my performance—I may, indeed, give credit to myself—but I have already turned back to my self-centeredness. And if I am not careful to remind myself that what the Spirit is doing is manifesting the goodness of Jesus in and through my particularity and not simply energizing me, then I will make the same mistake again.

Beyond this basic recognition, our moral identity in Christ becomes our *habitus* in prayer, particularly in prayer that is deliberately framed by trinitarian confession. I pray "Abba, Father" because I share in the sonship of Jesus; I do so because the Spirit co-testifies with my spirit that this address continues to be appropriate. I am baffled and horrified by the world around and in me, but I pray as one who inhabits the story of a crucified and risen Savior. In prayer I know that I am not of myself; I relate to God, in God, by God. My particularities remain—whether gender, hair color, or lineage—and they are different from yours, but we are united to the same person by the same person. In prayer we live this union. When asked, we may struggle to articulate what it involves, but its truth is one that we live. God has involved himself with us, and in prayer he involves us with himself.

Virtue, Discipline, and Psychology: Do They Have a Place in Christian Moral Identity?

Does this account of Christian moral identity leave any room for the practices of formation and discipline that are commonly part of our discipleship culture? The question will occur to readers because much of what I have written might suggest that they do not. Actually, I think they do, but they must be properly framed by union with Christ; it is when they are dislocated from this that they become problematic.

Paul forces us to think about salvation relationally, and relationships take effort. Part of that effort is a willingness to order our lives in such a way that the other person sometimes enjoys our undivided attention. Following a regular pattern of prayer and Scripture reading—what is often called a "quiet time"—or attending worship and seeking the oversight of other Christians can be invaluable to the development of our relationship with God in Christ. Married friends of mine regularly have a date night, an evening that they jealously protect as time to spend with each other, devoted to reminding each other of their love. To do so involves discipline, a commitment to preventing other things from encroaching on that time, but the discipline is distinctly relational. Similarly, being married involves certain disciplines about our relationships with other people: we cannot allow ourselves to do certain things or to think of other people in certain ways. We observe boundaries and limits because to cross those lines would compromise the relationship. And in important ways, this is "appetitive": our relationship with the other person redefines the way we allow our appetites to function. Because of our relationship with that person, we do not allow our appetite to possess or to consume things that are no longer beneficial. We train those appetites so that they feed our relationship and do not compromise it. This is discipline positively understood.

But we must be clear: it is the person who is to be the object of our attention and the reason for our discipline. If we treat a quiet time of reading Scripture as an end in itself, rather than as an exercise in listening to God, or if we treat scheduled fellowship events as the basis in themselves for Christian growth, we have lost sight of that vital point. We can enjoy these practices for the wrong reasons—taking pleasure in the acquisition of new knowledge, drawing on the social energy of a fellowship group, and feeling affirmed by our religious habits, all while directing none of our attention toward Jesus himself. And if we compartmentalize Jesus within one bit of this, losing sight of the fact that he is the mediator of everything, then everything else will become distorted. If I approach the OT, for example, as something I read to learn about God's commandments for how I am to live my life, rather than as something in which I seek to listen to Christ and understand what his presence in my life will look like, I have fallen into the trap of Pharisaism. What is striking about Paul's account of Christian growth is that, at every turn, it is directed toward Jesus as the one *in* whom the apostle's Christian identity is growing. That and that alone makes sense of his otherwise bizarre expression, "For to me to live is Christ" (Phil. 1:21).

This also means that when we speak of virtue, we must always do so in a carefully Christian way. It is a good thing that the language of virtue and character has come to be important again within evangelicalism, since it refocuses the discourse of Christian ethics onto the moral identity of the Christian and does not abstract the performance of obedience from this. Furthermore, it recognizes that our character is wrapped up with our appetites; it takes seriously the extent to which our identity is dynamically affected by the ways that we desire to relate to things. But if we do not immediately define that identity as one that emerges in union with Christ and qualify the way we speak of the Christian self to reflect this, we run the risk of making virtue into a kind of moral heroism. It is never heroism; it is participation. That is why it always involves prayer. Christian virtue is a distinctively eccentric thing.[4]

For the same reason, we need to be careful how we seek to incorporate the insights of psychology or the cognitive science of religion into our practices of discipleship. Again, it is essentially a good thing that such areas of study have become popular within evangelicalism. Aside from anything else, they acknowledge that our experience of discipleship is always embodied and that the bodies in question react and interact with circumstances in predictable ways, including at the level of psychology. Their findings are enormously helpful for how we understand the habitual dimension of our patterns of behavior and how these can be disrupted. For both the pastoral and the exegetical task, this is invaluable. But it is noteworthy (if unsurprising) that the Christian appropriation of these studies is often closely connected to the renewal of interest in virtue. As with virtue theory, any attempts to bring the findings of such studies to bear on Christian formation must recognize the need to qualify carefully the way that we speak of the Christian person or the Christian self. In particular, we need to be careful not to "naturalize" the formation of the Christian, as if it

4. I borrow the language of "eccentricity" from David H. Kelsey, *Eccentric Existence*. It indicates not only that Christian virtue looks odd to the eyes of the world but also that it is centered on something outside of ourselves.

were something that can be analyzed and explained in purely natural or scientific terms. The indwelling presence of Jesus Christ realized by the Holy Spirit cannot be studied empirically, and his operations are never mechanistic.

Nurturing Our Identity and Growing Up into Him

Are there particular things that might be done to nourish proper Christian moral identity? That, of course, is a vital question for all of us as we seek to grow as Christians and to overcome our besetting sin. It is a particularly important question for Christian leaders. As noted in the previous section, personal discipline is important, provided it is rightly focused on the person of Jesus, but are there practices that we ought to prioritize within the church, practices that will help to nurture the identity of those who are united to Christ and to abrade the surrogate identities that we often inhabit?

The answer is that we continue to do what Christians have always done, but with constant care to understand the real significance of those actions. We baptize, we break bread, we pray, we worship, and we read. These practices can be mechanical for us or can be assimilated to our own culture (including the evangelical subculture). This is not a new thing: what Paul writes to the Corinthians shows clearly that they have misunderstood the sacraments of baptism and Eucharist, probably under the influence of Mediterranean culture rather than the gospel itself. Paul's response is to lead his churches back to understanding the sacraments properly and thereby understanding their own individual and collective identity.

When we baptize or witness a baptism, then, it is important to recognize that the symbolism points not to the individual becoming a new creature—their own "new self"—but to the individual participating in the new creation that is constituted in Jesus. It is important that our proclamation identify the new self as that of the one who clothes the individual, Jesus Christ himself. As we need to remind ourselves and those around us, baptism signifies that Jesus's personal history is now ours and that, consequently, his personal future is now ours. Similarly, when we perform the Eucharist, we collectively inhabit and perform a memory that defines our relationships with God, with one another, and with the world, and we do so in a way that locates our experience of participation between incarnation and parousia. If we practice these sacraments knowingly, they define us and do so in a way that resists factionalism and individualism.

In prayer and in worship, the relationally constituted character of our Christian self emerges and is expressed. I manifest the truth that I am not "of myself" or "unto myself," that I am not the center of my own existence. Rather, I exist in the one whom I address, to whom I pray, and this reality is shared with all who pray in this way. In prayer my particular self—the things that are unique to me and that distinguish me from you—locates itself deliberately in Christ, reminding itself of the hidden presence of his Spirit. It is difficult to do so, to be sure. I groan and cry and need the Spirit's help if I am to testify that I am a child of God, but it is in prayer and worship that I experience my particularity being determined by his.

Even our acts of reading Scripture need to be defined in these personal terms. The language of Colossians captures this nicely, framed within the context of worship, and needs no further comment: "Let the word of Christ dwell in you richly, teaching and admonishing one another in all wisdom, singing psalms and hymns and spiritual songs, with thankfulness in your hearts to God" (Col. 3:16).

Legalism, Self-Righteousness, and Symbolic Capital

A pivotal part of our discussion in this book has concerned legalism and self-righteousness. We tend to use these terms as if the problem in question affects other people, not ourselves. When we think of legalism, we tend to think of either a card-carrying commitment to salvation by works or a traditional morality that simply seems out of date. When we think of self-righteousness, we tend to think of people who are smug and consider themselves morally superior to others. In truth, though, the words label problems that are much closer to home for each of us. Self-righteousness in Paul's discourse is simply a way of thinking about righteousness as something that can be associated with one's life or conduct and that can contribute to one's status as symbolic capital, regardless of whether one thinks of it in such terms. It is a righteousness that I associate with my self, in contrast to a righteousness that I enjoy because of my association with another self, Jesus. As such, one can be relatively humble and self-effacing but still be self-righteous, because whatever moral credibility we believe ourselves to have we associate with ourselves.

This way of thinking about righteousness is a function of a particular way of thinking about the self as an agent and a particular way of thinking about moral performance in relation to status. If I consider myself to be the one who performs good actions—or if others so consider me—then that performance can contribute to my status within the community: I can be an "upstanding member of the church," and if my performance appears to be better than that of others, then I can move from being a member to being a leader. My performance of morality has been "commodified": it has been turned into a symbolic commodity or social capital by which my worth and status are evaluated. That social capital affects the way that we assume we will be evaluated by other people and perhaps also the way that we think we will be evaluated by God.

Legalism is not really a Pauline word, but it helpfully labels a way of thinking about the moral life that involves the wrong use of the law. It sees obedience to the law as something that is performed by me, with the moral accomplishment becoming my capital. The problem is not an assumption that perfect performance of the law is the key to being saved. Instead, it is an assumption that I am the competent agent of obedience, whose status within God's community is materially linked to my performance.

Once this is grasped, we can see why legalism and self-righteousness are perennial existential problems for Christians, just as they were for Paul and the Pharisees and, later, for Peter and the circumcision group in Galatia. If sin, as it has been classically defined, is an "inward turn" by which we make our self the most important thing in our world, then this way of thinking about moral goodness—as something that my self does—will always be seductive, perhaps subliminally, and all too easily married to our religious life. The only antidote to it is a proper understanding of how the Christian self is constituted in union with Christ, something that dismantles the idea that "I" am the one who autonomously performs obedience and who can be credited with the social capital that it purchases.

But here is the point where our popular theology can be so problematic. Our emphasis on substitutionary atonement, as good as it is in itself, can leave us thinking of the place of Jesus in our salvation as principally associated with forgiveness purchased through his place-taking. When we think of Jesus as "Savior," we really mean that he is the one who saves us from punishment. The gospel here is narrowed to a transaction by which we are delivered from divine wrath, with this dislocated from a thicker account of the gospel that understands it as the whole answer to the whole problem of sin. The gospel of Jesus Christ is the answer to the enslaving, destructive power of sin, bringing freedom and healing and not just forgiveness. The work of the Spirit to transform is not a consequence of the gospel but is part of that gospel, and it is as thoroughly determined by the identity of Jesus Christ as is the cross. If we miss this by representing the Spirit as one who works in his own way to lead us to our own personal fulfillment, to become our own individual new creation, then our account of the gospel is mistaken, and we are vulnerable to the problems of legalism and self-righteousness. We will see the Spirit as one who helps us to do what we previously could not do ourselves, rather than seeing him as the one who helps us to inhabit Christ and become Christ's members.

This way of thinking about legalism and self-righteousness, or the problem of "works," also allows a different way through the mass of NT scholarship that has sought to address the perceived deficiency in Protestant accounts of justification by faith. By understanding legalism and self-righteousness as manifesting the instinctive or subliminal pursuit of social or symbolic capital, which gives the self a sense of status in relation to other people and in relation to God, we move past the problems associated with popular accounts of "salvation by works" (which don't really work as descriptions of ancient Judaism) without having to sacrifice more classical notions of righteousness and imputation. The key is that we have identified the problem at work in Pharisaism or in the Galatian heresy not as a flawed understanding of the law but as a flawed understanding of the self as a moral agent.

This takes us into territory different from that of N. T. Wright and other representatives of the New Perspective. For Wright, the problem embodied by the Pharisees and the Galatians involved using the law as a means of establishing (and sharpening) the boundaries between the people of God and the rest of humanity, thus breaking the true purpose of Israel's election and the giving of the law itself, which was to bring God's restorative blessing to the whole world. When Paul speaks of justification in Christ, Wright understands this to mean something different from the classical notion of imputed righteousness: instead, it indicates membership in God's covenant people, something that is now constituted by relationship to Jesus, not by relationship to the law, and that is open to the world. The approach I have taken here affirms elements of this, by seeing the performance of obedience as something that generates symbolic capital by which our status as "insiders" is affirmed to ourselves, to our peers, and to God. This may not be the result of deliberate or conscious effort on our part. Rather, it is wrapped up in our constitution, our flesh as Paul calls it, and operates deep in our psyche. Such social capital is acquired by the one who acts: it is a righteousness that is "mine." This assumes that I am both competent to act in such a creditable way and am the one who should be so credited, because "I" am the moral agent. Paul's account of righteousness in Christ opposes this entirely by recognizing that "I" have no such natural competency and that the goodness that I do as a believer is done through the indwelling presence of Christ. "I" can never be credited with righteousness, because that "I" no longer lives; it is now the I-in-Christ who lives, and it is Christ-in-me who works. The righteousness is his; I enjoy it because I share in him. The imputation of righteousness, then, is not a cold concept of credit sheets or bank statements but one of personal union: the righteousness of Christ inhabits me because Christ inhabits me, and I inhabit him.

The same affirmation stands over against any way of thinking about Christian righteousness that minimizes the importance of its actual manifestation in our lives. As we noted in the introduction, another strand of NT scholarship has seen any emphasis on the moral transformation of the individual believer to be inconsistent with a proper emphasis on grace, even redefining "faith" lest it be seen as a work that in some sense conditions the way God relates to us. Behind this lies a particular way of thinking about grace that emphasizes its priority and non-reciprocity: salvation is a free gift[5] that is given to those who cannot give any reciprocal return to God for it. It is given not to those who can return the investment but to those who are undeserving. As we noted in the introduction, such a way of thinking about the gift as "non-reciprocal" has recently been criticized by John Barclay.[6] He notes its failure to recognize the ways in which Paul presents the divine gift as something that is given to the unfitting but that brings about change in them. The gift is given to the "unfitting," but it brings about a "fittingness." The point that I make here builds on this observation and takes it further: precisely because the gift involves union with Jesus, whose righteousness now actively inhabits our limbs through the Spirit, it will manifest itself in a transformed life.

Love, Obedience, and Christian Unity

The transformation of our lives through the presence of Christ must manifest itself in the practices of love. He is love, and it is Love that now inhabits us and that we, in turn, inhabit. Our rendering of new obedience to God is a manifestation of the Son's love for the Father but also of the Father's love for the Son and for those to whom the Son is united. As we saw in Rom. 8, the Father involves us in the reality of providence. He makes it possible for us to serve him, to cry "Abba Father," and to eventually hear the words "Well done, good and faithful servant" (Matt. 25:23).

While this love must now define all that we do, it should manifest itself distinctively within the fellowship of the body of Christ, the church. Although we did not look in depth at 1 Cor. 13, Paul's famous description of love, we looked at the chapters leading up to it, which

5. The very expression "free gift" is used in the translation of the underlying words for "gift" (*dōrēma, charisma*) in the ESV and some other versions, but it is (somewhat ironically) an overly dynamic and theologically determined translation of the Greek words. They mean simply "gift," and it is the context that indicates the distinctive way in which Paul develops this idea.

6. Barclay, *Paul and the Gift*.

affirm that our identity in Christ is a collective one. We are united to Christ, and in Christ we are united to one another. Our symbolic enactments of this new identity portray this truth: there is one loaf, one cup, one Spirit from which we have all been made to drink, one Lord, one faith, one baptism. The unity of the church is a function of our union with the one God through the one mediator.

In reality, of course, the manifestation of this love within the fellowship will be flawed by the persistence of sin. The church will continue to be the place where the war of flesh and spirit takes place. We have highlighted something important in the course of this book, though, which is that our practices of disunity may be a function of our problematic theology. If we lose sight of union with Christ as the basis for all Christian identity, then we lose sight of the real significance of Paul's statements concerning our unity in Christ: "There is neither Jew nor Greek, there is neither slave nor free, there is no male and female, for you are all one in Christ Jesus" (Gal. 3:28). Once we have done that, we will lose sight of the fact that Christian unity is an essential function of our collective participation in Christ, and we will begin to redefine unity as something that emerges from our doctrinal agreement or ecclesial practices. Then we begin to subdivide the body. We need to remind ourselves of the shocking truth that those with whom we disagree are as united to Jesus Christ in the body of Christ as we are. That doesn't make it any less important that we argue about what constitutes good theology or good Christian practice. Actually, it makes it more important, because it is driven by love for fellow believers.

I am going to take the risk of offering a particularly provocative example of this. Much of the debate around same-sex relationships or LGBTI identity within the church has been marked by an initial polarization involving labels. For conservatives, this often involves stating that those advocating a position other than their own are either "not really Christians" or are not "Bible-believing Christians," for it is simply unthinkable to them that a fellow Christian would advocate the nontraditional position. I am raising this not in order to take a side in that debate but rather to highlight that this labeling effectively allows the Christians in question to dismiss the others and cease caring for them as fellow members of the body. These debates have been public and have publicly appeared to be rather loveless; they are conversations between enemies. And, effectively, they have killed any real dialogue. The conversation has stopped shortly after the exercise in labeling, because there is no reason for it to continue. By contrast, if we begin with the affirmation that these are fellow believers, we have no excuse to walk away from the conversation and no excuse to conduct it in a way that is anything other than loving. Far from glossing over the substance of the issues, it makes them all the more important. In the process, we may find our own views changing, or they may become reinforced as we consider the weaknesses of alternatives, but we always consider other members of the body with the generosity that comes from love: "Love is patient and kind; love does not envy or boast; it is not arrogant or rude. It does not insist on its own way; it is not irritable or resentful; it does not rejoice at wrongdoing, but rejoices with the truth. Love bears all things, believes all things, hopes all things, endures all things" (1 Cor. 13:4–7).

However, the attitude of love involves a proper recognition of Christian identity and mutual obligation as being grounded in our union with Christ, and here perhaps is the problem that has compromised these debates. If our account of Christian identity lacks a proper emphasis on union with Christ, then it will be defined more naturally in terms of the content of our beliefs and the agreement of our practices. To belong to a group, we then need to agree with one another. Those who do not agree simply do not belong. Consequently, we feel no need to love them as we ought. This is a stark example, but every day at a more mundane level, Christians deny the unity of the body by defining its limits according to their beliefs rather than according to union with Christ.

Beyond Imitation: Trinitarian Theology and Participatory Ethics

I began this book with some comments on how an account of Christian moral identity that takes seriously the concept of union with Christ differs from popular evangelical accounts of the gospel. Let me close with some reflections on the trinitarian framework of that identity, drawing together some of the themes that have emerged throughout the book and considering them in relation to both popular evangelicalism and academic biblical studies.

Union with Christ and its bearing on our moral identity is grounded on an incarnational theology that acknowledges the two natures of Christ, considered in ontological terms. Jesus *is* God, and he *is* man; he *is* the Creator, and he *is* a creature. Within the person of the mediator, these two natures are united, and as such he has a dual kinship that allows him, uniquely, to be the mediator of the covenant between God and his people. He shares a kinship with God the Father as God the Son, and he shares a kinship with us as our brother. The union itself involves the Holy Spirit, not as the one who constitutes the divinity of Christ (as someone like James Dunn would argue),[7] but as the one through whom the Son acts upon the creaturely nature that he has united to himself. The mediator, by the activity of the Spirit, offers perfect creaturely obedience to the Father. Because of our kinship with him, we can share in this, and this sharing is more than just representational or symbolic: it is real. For the same Spirit—his Spirit—acts on our flesh in a corresponding way to bring about a transformation within us. In the Spirit, he inhabits us; by the Spirit, we inhabit him.

This incarnational account, in turn, rests on a properly conceived account of the Trinity, one that does not lose sight of the essential simplicity of God. Canonically, as Katherine Sonderegger has recently emphasized, we know God as one long before we know him as three, and the shape of this disclosure is important.[8] Fundamentally, it prevents us from seeing the Spirit as an independent energy working to make us into better versions of ourselves. It demands instead that we see him as the one working to realize the identity of the Son within us, and the Son himself is seen to be God working reconciliation by making himself present with and in us.

Within academic biblical studies, such categories are, for the most part, alien. Even the conservative biblical studies that have defended early high Christology have largely shifted toward using the language

---

7. See under "Galatians 4: Adoption and Christian Identity" in chap. 5.
8. Sonderegger, *Doctrine of God*.

of "binitarianism," in which what is defended is the divinity of Jesus as an object of worship.[9] The place of the Spirit is largely neglected.[10] This has a parallel in the studies that are less concerned with Christology and more concerned with soteriology. Even John Barclay's magnificent study *Paul and the Gift*—which really asserts a fairly traditional understanding of justification by faith and argues that Luther's theology was actually a careful piece of recontextualization rather than the anachronism it has often been called—devotes only a few pages to the Spirit,[11] which seems a strange decision when we consider how prominent the Spirit has been in our own reflections. More widely, the Spirit is either neglected or is seen as some kind of psychological phenomenon.

This has had a seriously distortive effect on accounts of soteriology. With only a few exceptions,[12] most of the scholars working on so-called participatory accounts of salvation read the material in a way that allows no real traction in the lives of believers. This is despite the fact that many see themselves as offering accounts that are theologically astute and rightly shaped by the preeminence of Christology. But it is a Christology that has been dislocated from its classical trinitarian framework and lacks, in particular, a robust understanding of theology proper—what God is in himself—and a robust understanding of the

9. See, e.g., Hurtado, *Lord Jesus Christ*.

10. There are a few notable exceptions to this. Gordon Fee has devoted a number of works to the study of the Spirit, including his *Paul, the Spirit, and the People of God* and his magisterial *God's Empowering Presence*. John R. Levison has also made important contributions to the study of the Spirit that are sensitive both to the background issues in Second Temple Judaism and to the philosophical currents of modern scholarship. See his *Filled with the Spirit* and his *Inspired*. As noted at several points already in this book, James Dunn has also been one of the few scholars to give the Holy Spirit an appropriate proportion in his work, though his representation of the Spirit's role in the incarnation is one I consider to be problematic.

11. Barclay, *Paul and the Gift*, 425–28, 439–42. While the Spirit is mentioned in other parts of the book, these are the only parts that really involve sustained discussion of his role. Having said this, Barclay is keenly sensitive to the fact that Paul's representation of the Spirit demands a distinctive account of Christian moral agency: "The presence of Christ within as 'the Spirit' means that believer agency is by no means self-generated or independent, let alone autonomous. . . . At the same time, Paul has no hesitation in speaking of believers as agents." *Paul and the Gift*, 441.

12. Notably Beverly Gaventa ("Shape of the 'I'") and Susan Eastman (*Paul and the Person*).

Spirit as the one by whom God acts upon creation to bring about the gospel's promised transformation.

But here is the rub: Is evangelical theology, particularly in its popular forms, much better? How often have you been in contexts where there is serious engagement with two-natures Christology or discussion of the problems with monophysitism? How often have you talked about divine simplicity? The problem is that our evangelicalism is much more compromised by modernity and its fashions than we often recognize and is much more cultural and much less theological than we often think it to be. The decline of serious theology is, I suspect, a big part of the reason why we often operate with an account of Christian moral identity that is rather different from the one I have been outlining here.

In particular, I think this decline is behind the rather thin account of imitation operative in the approach that asks, "What would Jesus do?" This approach assigns an admirable priority to the person of Jesus and to the gospel narratives in which his actions are described but does not frame these adequately in relation to trinitarian theology; it lacks an account of the Spirit that properly relates his work to the identity of Christ and lacks a soteriology that properly understands the Son's mediatorial role.

Aside from the overly simplistic notion of Christian agency that it generally involves, which is the one that I have criticized throughout this book, the approach cannot meaningfully negotiate the gulf between our personal and moral particularities and those of Jesus of Nazareth. For a husband to ask "What would Jesus do?" in relation to the internal challenges of a marriage is problematic because Jesus was unmarried. For his wife to ask the same thing is also problematic, but even more so, because Jesus is of a different gender from her. Such particularities multiply the more that we consider them. Put simply, the gospel narratives can never give us all the resources we need to navigate the moral or ethical decisions that we face. We need a fuller engagement with Scripture to sustain such reflection, properly informed by our moral relationship to Jesus. This does not minimize the importance of the gospel narratives or detract from the need for a certain kind of imitation, but it sets these in a richer framework and asks the question in a subtly different way: "How does the acting presence of Jesus bear upon this situation as his Spirit works in and through us?" or "How do I inhabit the goodness of Jesus by his Spirit?"[13]

In the end, this must also lead us to a thicker and more theologically rounded account of the life of Christ's church as his embodied presence in the world. The church is not simply a community that has been saved from punishment by God, not simply a community that now worships and serves God, and not simply a community that is marked by an imitative resemblance to Jesus Christ. The community embodies the life and goodness of Jesus himself as it is constituted by the presence of his Spirit. It inhabits the goodness of Jesus, even as his goodness inhabits it. This is why, in the end, the flesh that wars against the Spirit will not be victorious. This is why sin will not be the final defining reality of my life or of yours or of the body of saints to which we belong. The final defining reality of our lives and our church is the potent goodness of Jesus Christ.

---

13. This theological deficiency seems to me to be a problem with Burridge, *Imitating Jesus*.

Bibliography

Allen, Michael. *Sanctification*. New Studies in Dogmatics. Grand Rapids: Zondervan, 2017.

Arnold, Clinton. *The Colossian Syncretism: The Interface between Christianity and Folk Belief at Colossae*. WUNT 2.77. Tübingen: Mohr Siebeck, 1995.

Banks, Iain. *The Bridge*. London: Macmillan, 1986. Repr., London: Abacus, 2007.

Barclay, John M. G. *Paul and the Gift*. Grand Rapids: Eerdmans, 2015.

Barclay, John M. G., and Simon J. Gathercole. *Divine and Human Agency in Paul and His Cultural Environment*. LNTS 335. London: T&T Clark, 2006.

Barr, James. "'*Abbā* Isn't 'Daddy.'" *Journal of Theological Studies* 39 (1988): 28–47.

Bauckham, Richard. *God Crucified: Monotheism and Christology in the New Testament*. Grand Rapids: Eerdmans, 1999.

Billings, J. Todd. *Calvin, Participation, and the Gift: The Activity of Believers in Union with Christ*. Changing Paradigms in Historical and Systematic Theology. Oxford: Oxford University Press, 2008.

———. *Union with Christ: Reframing Theology and Ministry for the Church*. Grand Rapids: Baker Academic, 2011.

Bird, Michael F., and Preston M. Sprinkle, eds. *The Faith of Jesus Christ: Exegetical, Biblical, and Theological Studies*. Peabody, MA: Hendrickson, 2009.

Bitner, Bradley J. *Paul's Political Strategy in 1 Corinthians 1–4: Constitution and Covenant.* SNTSMS 163. Cambridge: Cambridge University Press, 2015.

Blade Runner. Directed by Ridley Scott. 1982; Burbank, CA: Warner Home Video, 2007. DVD.

Blade Runner 2049. Directed by Denis Villeneuve. Burbank, CA: Warner Bros. Entertainment, 2017. Blu-ray Disc.

Burke, Kenneth. *Language as Symbolic Action: Essays on Life, Literature, and Method.* Berkeley: University of California Press, 1966.

———. *Permanence and Change: An Anatomy of Purpose.* Berkeley: University of California Press, 1954.

Burridge, Richard. *Imitating Jesus: An Inclusive Approach to New Testament Ethics.* Grand Rapids: Eerdmans, 2007.

———. *What Are the Gospels? A Comparison with Graeco-Roman Biography.* Cambridge: Cambridge University Press, 1992.

Campbell, Douglas A. "The Current Crisis: The Capture of Paul's Gospel by Methodological Arianism." Pages 37–48 in *Beyond Old and New Perspectives on Paul: Reflections on the Work of Douglas Campbell.* Edited by Chris Tilling. Eugene, OR: Cascade, 2014.

———. *The Deliverance of God: An Apocalyptic Rereading of Justification in Paul.* Grand Rapids: Eerdmans, 2009.

———. "Douglas Campbell's Response to Scott Hafemann." Pages 230–33 in *Beyond Old and New Perspectives on Paul: Reflections on the Work of Douglas Campbell.* Edited by Chris Tilling. Eugene, OR: Cascade, 2014.

———. "Rereading Paul's ΔΙΚΑΙΟ-Language." Pages 196–213 in *Beyond Old and New Perspectives on Paul: Reflections on the Work of Douglas Campbell.* Edited by Chris Tilling. Eugene, OR: Cascade, 2014.

Carson, D. A., Peter T. O'Brien, and Mark A. Seifrid, eds. *Justification and Variegated Nomism.* 2 vols. Grand Rapids: Baker Academic, 2001–4.

Chester, Stephen. *Reading Paul with the Reformers: Reconciling Old and New Perspectives.* Grand Rapids: Eerdmans, 2017.

Croasmun, Matthew. *The Emergence of Sin: The Cosmic Tyrant in Romans.* Oxford: Oxford University Press, 2017.

Crossan, J. D. *The Historical Jesus: The Life of a Mediterranean Jewish Peasant.* San Francisco: HarperOne, 1993.

Davis, Joshua B., and Douglas K. Harink, eds. *Apocalyptic and the Future of Theology: With and beyond J. Louis Martyn.* Eugene, OR: Cascade, 2012.

Dick, Philip K. *Do Androids Dream of Electric Sheep?* Garden City, NY: Doubleday, 1968.

Dobroruka, Vicente. *Second Temple Pseudepigraphy: A Cross-Cultural Comparison of Apocalyptic Texts and Related Jewish Literature.* Ekstasis: Religious Experience from Antiquity to the Middle Ages 4. Berlin: de Gruyter, 2014.

Dunn, James. *Christology in the Making: A New Testament Inquiry into the Origins of the Doctrine of the Incarnation.* 2nd ed. London: SCM, 1989.

———. *Jesus and the Spirit: A Study of the Religious and Charismatic Experience of Jesus and the First Christians as Reflected in the New Testament.* London: SCM, 1975.

———. "Jesus—Flesh and Spirit: An Exposition of Romans 1.3–4." *Journal of Theological Studies* 24 (1973): 40–68.

———. "Rediscovering the Spirit." *Expository Times* 84 (1972): 7–12.

Dunn, James D. G., and James P. Mackey. *New Testament Theology in Dialogue.* Biblical Foundations in Theology. London: SPCK, 1987.

Eastman, Susan. *Paul and the Person: Reframing Paul's Anthropology.* Grand Rapids: Eerdmans, 2017.

Engberg-Pedersen, Troels. *Cosmology and the Self in the Apostle Paul: The Material Spirit.* Oxford: Oxford University Press, 2010.

———. *Paul and the Stoics.* Edinburgh: T&T Clark, 2000.

Fee, Gordon. *God's Empowering Presence: The Holy Spirit in the Letters of Paul.* Peabody, MA: Hendrickson, 1994. Repr., Grand Rapids: Baker Academic, 2011.

———. *Paul, the Spirit, and the People of God.* Peabody, MA: Hendrickson, 1996. Repr., Grand Rapids: Baker Academic, 2011.

Ferguson, Sinclair. *The Whole Christ: Legalism, Antinomianism, and Gospel Assurance—Why the Marrow Controversy Still Matters.* Wheaton: Crossway, 2016.

Foster, Paul. *Colossians.* London: Bloomsbury, 2016.

Frederick, John. *The Ethics of the Enactment and Reception of Cruciform Love: A Comparative Lexical, Conceptual, Exegetical, and Theological Study of Colossians 3:1–17.* WUNT. Tübingen: Mohr Siebeck, forthcoming.

Garcia, Mark. *Life in Christ: Union with Christ and Twofold Grace in Calvin's Theology.* Studies in Christian History and Thought. Carlisle, UK: Paternoster, 2008. Repr., Eugene, OR: Wipf & Stock, 2008.

Gathercole, Simon. *Where Is Boasting? Early Jewish Soteriology and Paul's Response in Romans 1–5.* Grand Rapids: Eerdmans, 2003.

Gaventa, Beverly R. "The Shape of the 'I': The Psalter, the Gospel, and the Speaker in Romans 7." Pages 77–92 in *Apocalyptic Paul: Cosmos and Anthropos in Roman 5–8.* Edited by Beverly R. Gaventa. Waco: Baylor University Press, 2013.

Goldman, William. *The Princess Bride.* New York: Macmillan, 1973. 2nd ed., New York: Bloomsbury, 1999.

Gorman, Michael. *Cruciformity: Paul's Narrative Spirituality of the Cross.* Grand Rapids: Eerdmans, 2001.

———. *Inhabiting the Cruciform God: Kenosis, Justification, and Theosis in Paul's Narrative Soteriology.* Grand Rapids: Eerdmans, 2009.

Hafemann, Scott. "Reading Paul's ΔIKAIO-Language: A Response to Douglas Campbell's 'Rereading Paul's ΔIKAIO-Language.'" Pages 214–29 in *Beyond Old and New Perspectives on Paul: Reflections on the Work of Douglas Campbell.* Edited by Chris Tilling. Eugene, OR: Cascade, 2014.

Hartman, Lars. "'Into the Name of Jesus': A Suggestion concerning the Earliest Meaning of the Phrase." *New Testament Studies* 20 (1974): 432–40.

Hauerwas, Stanley. *Character and the Christian Life: A Study in Theological Ethics.* San Antonio: Trinity University Press, 1975.

Hauerwas, Stanley, and Charles Pinches. "Virtue Christianly Considered." Pages 287–304 in *Christian Theism and Moral Philosophy.* Edited by M. D. Beaty, C. D. Fisher, and M. T. Nelson. Macon, GA: Mercer University Press, 1998.

Hays, Richard, B. *The Faith of Jesus Christ: The Narrative Substructure of Galatians 3:1–4:11.* SBLDS 56. Atlanta: SBL Press, 1983. 2nd ed., Grand Rapids: Eerdmans, 2001.

———. *First Corinthians.* Interpretation. Louisville: Westminster John Knox, 1997.

Herdt, Jennifer A. *Putting on Virtue: The Legacy of the Splendid Vices.* Chicago: University of Chicago Press, 2008.

Hurtado, Larry. *Lord Jesus Christ: Devotion to Jesus in Earliest Christianity.* Grand Rapids: Eerdmans, 2003.

Jensen, Matt. *The Gravity of Sin: Augustine, Luther and Barth on homo incurvatus in se.* London: T&T Clark, 2007.

Käsemann, Ernst. "The Beginnings of Christian Theology." *Journal for Theology and the Church* 6 (1969): 17–46. Translation of "Die Anfänge christlicher Theologie." *Zeitschrift für Theologie und Kirche* 57 (1960): 162–85.

———. *Commentary on Romans.* Translated and edited by Geoffrey W. Bromiley. Grand Rapids: Eerdmans, 1980.

Keith, Chris. "Social Memory Theory and Gospels Research: The First Decade." *Early Christianity* 6 (2015): 354–76, 517–42.

Keller, Tim. *The Freedom of Self-Forgetfulness: The Path to True Christian Joy.* New York: 10Publishing, 2012.

———. *Prayer: Experiencing Awe and Intimacy with God.* London: Hodder & Stoughton, 2014.

Kelsey, David H. *Eccentric Existence: A Theological Anthropology.* Louisville: Westminster John Knox, 2009.

Kilby, Karen. "Perichoresis and Projection: Problems with Social Doctrines of the Trinity." *New Blackfriars* 81 (2000): 432–45.

Letham, Robert. *Union with Christ: In Scripture, History, and Theology.* Phillipsburg, NJ: P&R, 2011.

Levison, John R. *Filled with the Spirit.* Grand Rapids: Eerdmans, 2009.

———. *Inspired: The Holy Spirit and the Mind of Faith.* Grand Rapids: Eerdmans, 2013.

Lietzmann, Hans. *Mass and Lord's Supper: A Study in the History of the Liturgy.* Translated by Dorothea Holman Gessner Reeve. Leiden: Brill, 1979.

Macaskill, Grant. "Incarnational Ontology and the Theology of Participation in Paul." Pages 87–102 in *"In Christ" in Paul: Explorations in Paul's Theology of Union and Participation.* Edited by Kevin J. Vanhoozer, Constantine Campbell, and Michael Thate. WUNT 2.384. Tübingen: Mohr Siebeck, 2014.

———. "Review Article: *The Deliverance of God.*" *Journal for the Study of the New Testament* 34 (2011): 150–61.

———. *Union with Christ in the New Testament.* Oxford: Oxford University Press, 2013.

MacIntyre, Alasdair. *After Virtue: A Study in Moral Theory.* Notre Dame, IN: University of Notre Dame Press, 1981.

Malina, Bruce. *The New Testament World: Insights from Cultural Anthropology.* Atlanta: John Knox, 1981.

Martyn, J. Louis. "De-apocalypticizing Paul: An Essay Focused on *Paul and the Stoics*, by Troels Engberg-Pedersen." *Journal for the Study of the New Testament* 86 (2002): 61–102.

———. *Galatians: A New Translation with Introduction and Commentary.* New York: Doubleday, 1997.

Miller, Colin D. *The Practice of the Body of Christ: Human Agency in Pauline Thought after MacIntyre.* Princeton Theological Monograph Series. Eugene, OR: Pickwick, 2014.

Moltmann, Jürgen. *Theology of Hope: On the Ground and the Implications of a Christian Eschatology.* London: SCM, 1967.

Nikkanen, P. Markus. "Participation in Christ: Paul and Pre-Pauline Eucharistic Tradition." PhD diss., University of Aberdeen, 2018.

Porter, Stanley E., and Andrew Pitts. "Πίστις with a Preposition and Genitive Modifier: Lexical, Semantic, and Syntactic Considerations in the Πίστις Χριστοῦ Debate." Pages 33–53 in *The Faith of Jesus Christ: Exegetical, Biblical, and Theological Studies.* Edited by Michael F. Bird and Preston M. Sprinkle. Peabody, MA: Hendrickson, 2009.

Princess Bride, The. Directed by Rob Reiner. 1987; Beverly Hills, CA: Twentieth Century Fox Home Entertainment, 2017. Blu-ray Disc.

Ridderbos, Herman. *Paul: An Outline of His Theology.* Grand Rapids: Eerdmans, 1975.

Rosner, Brian. *Known by God: A Biblical Theology of Personal Identity.* Grand Rapids: Zondervan, 2017.

Sanders, E. P. *Paul and Palestinian Judaism: A Comparison of Patterns of Religion.* Minneapolis: Fortress, 1977.

Smith, J. Warren. "'Arian' Foundationalism or 'Athanasian' Apocalypticism: A Patristic Assessment." Pages 78–92 in *Beyond Old and New Perspectives on Paul: Reflections on the Work of Douglas Campbell.* Edited by Chris Tilling. Eugene, OR: Cascade, 2014.

Smith, James K. A. *Desiring the Kingdom: Worship, Worldview, and Cultural Formation.* Grand Rapids: Baker Academic, 2009.

———. *You Are What You Love: The Spiritual Power of Habit.* Grand Rapids: Brazos, 2016.

Sonderegger, Katherine. *The Doctrine of God.* Vol. 1 of *Systematic Theology.* Minneapolis: Fortress, 2015.

Spence, Alan. *Incarnation and Inspiration: John Owen and the Coherence of Christology.* London: T&T Clark, 2007.

Stendahl, Krister. "The Apostle Paul and the Introspective Conscience of the West." *Harvard Theological Review* 56 (1963): 199–215.

Swinton, John. *Dementia: Living in the Memories of God*. Grand Rapids: Eerdmans, 2012.

Tanner, Kathryn. *Jesus, Humanity and the Trinity: A Brief Systematic Theology*. Minneapolis: Fortress, 2001.

Taylor, Charles. *A Secular Age*. Cambridge, MA: Harvard University Press, 2007.

———. *The Sources of the Self: The Making of Modern Identity*. Cambridge: Cambridge University Press, 1989.

Tilling, Chris, ed., *Beyond Old and New Perspectives on Paul: Reflections on the Work of Douglas Campbell*. Eugene, OR: Cascade, 2014.

Torrance, J. B. "Covenant or Contract: A Study of the Theological Background of Worship in Seventeenth-Century Scotland." *Scottish Journal of Theology* 23 (1970): 51–76.

Westerholm, Stephen. *Perspectives Old and New on Paul: The "Lutheran" Paul and His Critics*. Grand Rapids: Eerdmans, 2004.

Wright, N. T. "4QMMT and Paul: Justification, 'Works,' and Eschatology." Pages 104–32 in *History and Exegesis: New Testament Essays in Honor of Dr. E. Earle Ellis for His 80th Birthday*. Edited by Sang-Won (Aaron) Son. London: T&T Clark, 2006.

———. *Jesus and the Victory of God*. London: SPCK, 1996.

———. "New Perspectives on Paul." Pages 243–64 in *Justification in Perspective: Historical Developments and Contemporary Challenges*. Edited by Bruce McCormack. Grand Rapids: Baker Academic, 2006.

———. *The New Testament and the People of God*. London: SPCK, 1992.

———. *Paul and the Faithfulness of God*. Minneapolis: Fortress, 2013.

———. *Virtue Reborn*. London: SPCK, 2010. Published in the US as *After You Believe: Why Christian Character Matters*. New York: HarperOne, 2010.

Ziegler, Philip. *Militant Grace: The Apocalyptic Turn and the Future of Christian Theology*. Grand Rapids: Baker Academic, 2018.

———. "Some Remarks on Apocalyptic in Modern Christian Theology." Pages 199–216 in *Paul and the Apocalyptic Imagination*. Edited by Ben C. Blackwell, John K. Goodrich, and Jason Maston. Minneapolis: Fortress, 2016.

Author Index

Scripture Index

156

Subject Index